INSIDER TIPS

100 Innovative Ways to Increase Profit

A Book Collaboration

from

Tracee Randall and Carol D. Neal

Atlanta Business Spotlight

DEDICATION

This book is dedicated to

Janice L. Dressler (1922-2016)

Anastasia Love Randall, born July 9, 2016

and to the thousands of brave souls who get up every day
and go out into the world to build their dreams.

CONTENTS

ACKNOWLEDGMENTS

We'd like to thank Lorna Rasmussen and ALL of the experts who answered the call to participate in this collaboration and share their experiences and expertise.

Special thanks to Ires Alliston, Taneka Badie and Laura Baker for sharing their special talents by creating amazing graphics and videos to promote the project.

Thank you to Robby and Ryan Randall for the cover designs, and for all their technical advice and support; and to Bobby Randall for his unfailing patience and understanding, and for keeping us well-fed and encouraged during the long hours of editing.

We thank our Atlanta Business Spotlight members and Xperience Connections community for keeping us motivated to seek and provide new opportunities, and we are grateful for the many mentors who have come into our lives and the #InsiderTips they have shared with us.

Finally we give thanks to God for letting us walk in #MiracleTerritory ...without Him none of the rest would be possible.

~ Tracee and Carol

Lorna Rasmussen

Lorna Rasmussen began her professional life as an award-winning documentary film producer. She taught at universities in Canada and the USA and later ran a commercial film production company with her husband. Making a complete career change after the birth of her son, Lorna bought a training franchise in which she taught clients how to set and achieve goals. She would say that her work was both fulfilling and meaningful but with all of her ventures she was never financially successful. That changed when she found the profession of Direct Selling/Network Marketing.

Lorna's story is compelling - at 48 she was about to lose everything. Ten years later she had made more than a million dollars and created a six figure residual income. In her 23 years in the direct sales world, tenacity and determination played an important role in her success. She has consistently earned a six figure income for the past 18 years. But above all she has lived the power of residual and leveraged income. "When I lost my house to a fire 10 years ago, I didn't work on my business for almost a year and then only part-time for the next 2 years. Because of the team I had created, I saw very little impact on my income."

In LegalShield, her Direct Sales company, Lorna has achieved one of the highest positions and is a member of the "Millionaire Club". While money is important, Lorna's major goal is to make a difference in people's lives. Working on her personal development through the teachings of Paul J. Meyer has really been the key. She now lives in Atenas, Costa Rica; Atlanta, GA and Alberta, Canada.

She is the co-author of a book on women's history, a contributor to "Build It Big", a how-to book by the Direct Selling Women's Alliance, as well as "Direct Selling Power". She was a contributor to "Guerilla Multi-Level Marketing" and is a co-author of "It's Time...for Network Marketing" edited by John Fogg. She is author of "The Absolute Best Way for Women to Make Money" and "The Absolute Best Way for African-American Women to Make Money" and is completing a new book entitled "Retire Rich: Even if You Haven't Planned for It, Saved for it and You're Running Out of Time". It will be available at the beginning of 2017.

More information on Lorna and her books can be found on her website: www.LornaRasmussen.com

For information on how LegalShield can help you with your business, go to www.successnetwork.org

Foreword

Lorna Rasmussen

There are two ways to learn about business – through your own mistakes or through the mistakes of others. Obviously, the first is the most expensive and painful. A sobering statistic for every want-to-be entrepreneur is that of all the businesses created, 95% are out of business within their first 5 years. To beat the odds and end up in the 5% that succeed, you must absolutely learn from the mistakes of others.

That is why this book is such an indispensable tool.

Like most people, when I started my first business three decades ago, I had the knowledge of and a passion for what I was offering to the world. But knowledge about the product or service of your business and even passion will only go so far. At some point you need to know the "business of your business".

What surprises people is how much you need to know about a diverse assortment of topics. From branding to marketing to legal issues, an entrepreneur has to be, if not an expert, at least knowledgeable. For those just starting a business this book will provide an invaluable guide to what is important as you prepare yourself for your undertaking. For those with a business they wish to grow, there are tips on everything from networking to branding.

Something I particularly like that this book acknowledges, is that people can go into business without having an earth-changing, original idea. They devote a whole area to Direct Selling and Network Marketing. In my book "The Absolute Best Way for Women to Make Money" I go through all the entrepreneurial ventures I attempted before finding the one where I really succeeded and that was Network Marketing. Even here there are tips that can make the difference between success and failure. This diverse and wide-ranging book covers this area as well.

I am impressed by the quality of the people brought together for this book and I know, as a reader, you will find their "tips" priceless. They have all, to a person, had tremendous success and this is a great introduction to what they can teach you. I also applaud and appreciate Tracee Randall and Carol Neal for their vision and commitment to bringing this book into a world of entrepreneurs who so desperately need it.

Read and absorb the content of this book. Learn not only from the mistakes but also the successes of others and build yourself a business that is lasting and successful. Be part of the 5% who succeed.

My Tip: Work on yourself as much as you work on your business. Become a student of personal development and get 1% better every day. Don't be afraid to fail and take every set back as an opportunity to learn and grow.

Tracee Randall

If you ask Tracee, she will tell you that the accomplishment she is most proud of is her 31+ year marriage to her husband Bobby, together raising 2 incredible sons, Robby and Ryan, and her adorable 4 Grandchildren. Together she and Bobby (along with her sons and daughter-in-love, Katrina) have owned several brick and mortar businesses and built million-dollar corporations in the service and relocation industries.

After overcoming food addiction, panic attacks and self-esteem issues, Tracee uses her experiences to empower other women to walk into the greatness that God has designed for them, addressing women's groups across the country, and has several published works in women's magazines. She is an author in the best-selling book series, "The Change—Insights Into Empowerment", and has released her own book, "The FASTest Way to God's Favor and Blessing." Her FASTing curriculum is designed to take people on a journey of fulfilling God's plan for their lives.

She is one of Georgia's foremost Wellness Coaches, and has created several workshops on the subject of wellness including "Get MAD About Cancer" and "Make Up Your Mind." She is recognized internationally as a speaker and works closely with the American Anti-Cancer Institute to educate families on the prevention of disease, and is the recipient of the esteemed Dr. Theodore Kalogris Humanitarian Award for her efforts in working with families with disease.

In 2007 she and her husband embarked in the direct sales industry, where they quickly made their mark as Ambassadors, traveling across the country teaching other distributors how to effectively build a profitable direct sales company. They have 14 years of experience in the industry, which she shares in online and in-person workshops created by Atlanta Business Spotlight for their #BeTheVoice training series.

Her programs are designed to empower the entrepreneur as well as corporations as she educates on team building, creating healthy relationships, and increasing profits from the sole proprietor to the large corporation. Audiences love her funny and entertaining style as she speaks boldly on every subject she attacks. Her workshops "Make Up Your Mind" and "H.A.T. Training—How to Attract Your Team" are designed to create strong goals and relationships that generate profits and change!

Tracee and her Atlanta Business Spotlight partner Carol Neal recently acquired the international women's networking organization, Xperience Connections. Founded by Bonnie Ross-Parker in 2002, Xperience Connections' mission is to empower women to become leaders in their area, and to expand their businesses through building relationships with other women. Tracee is the Chief Motivational Officer and is committed to expanding XC globally. For more information on this go to www.XperienceConnections.com.

Go to www.TraceeRandall.com and click on SUBSCRIBE for monthly tips on building your business AND free health tips and videos!
Email: Tracee@TraceeRandall.com
www.Facebook.com/TraceeSmithRandall
www.twitter.com/TraceeSRandall

See Tracee's #InsiderTips on pages 57, 71, 85, 97, 127, 153, 203, 235

Introduction

Tracee Randall

When I look back over my 30+ years as an entrepreneur and small business owner, I think about all the incredible people who were a part of my journey—the amazing like-minded people who sat down with me and gave me advice, helped me out of my messes, encouraged me when I was down, and inspired me to be the best that I could be. Behind every successful business man or woman there are always those who have gone before, cleared the path, paved the way.

We put this book collaborative together for multiple reasons. First of all, as small business owners having the opportunity to come together and collaborate with other successful entrepreneurs is priceless for those involved! I have known for many years that having my name on the front cover of a book (a well written, valuable book!) is priceless in moving my career forward, and have encouraged those around me to be published as well. But it is overwhelming for most small business owners to consider writing a full book, so a collaborative is a fabulous way to solve that issue—to come together with others and write a chapter or a portion of a book is brilliant, and I love giving others the opportunity to build themselves and their businesses! When thinking about the subject matter, we knew we wanted it to be a saleable commodity, and a project that brought value to the marketplace!

Most of my very best ideas come to me in the early morning hours, when the world around me is quiet and my mind can be open to thoughts and creativity abounds. I began to think about what is it that all small business owners need to know, what are the things that I wish I had known starting out in the direct sales industry, how does social media really work and how can I profit from it? I knew that I was an expert in some of these areas, but certainly not all of them—what would an expert on social media or branding tell me if they could give me 5-10 of their hottest, most profitable tips?? As these questions began to run through my head it occurred to me that if these tips were put together in one place, in one book, how beneficial that would be to every entrepreneur, every small business owner!

What if you were offered the opportunity to sit in the board room of 16 highly successful, affluent and dynamic business owners and entrepreneurs to hear what goes on behind closed doors? What if you were invited to a VIP round table and were able to listen in on that conversation? This book contains 100 tips revealed by these experts. It will open the door for you to increase your profits! Are you looking to start a new business? Are you interested in expanding your center of influence through networking? This book is full of innovative and powerful tips from some of the top networking experts in the world today! Are you completely baffled by what to post, what not to post, and HOW to increase sales using social media? Our experts in social media—Facebook, Twitter and LinkedIn--will give you their hottest time-saving tips. Are you part of the direct sales industry and can't figure out why your team isn't growing? Look no further, we have some of the top income earners in the industry in this book sharing tips that you won't learn anywhere else. This book is a gold mine for the small business owner or entrepreneur!

This is not a book that will sit on your shelf unread. We encourage you to read it through, then go back and highlight the tips that will help you NOW—in whatever area you need help in—and then go back again and again, perfecting your craft, creating new habits and utilizing the tips that benefit you the most! And then, SHARE this book with your colleagues, team members, referral partners, and mentors. What an incredible gift this would be for a new team member or as a thank you to a referral partner!

Shortcut your way to success! And who knows, next time YOU may be the expert!!

Carol D. Neal, CCBE/MPCE

Carol Neal is passionate about connecting people...she sees the world as a giant puzzle and loves to fit the right resources together. Her goal in any networking meeting is to match people up and make great referrals. Her motto is "Let Your Light Shine", and she believes her purpose is to help others be the best that they can be by providing inspiration, opportunities, resources and connections to help them succeed.

Carol was raised in Ohio and went to college in Mississippi before getting married and moving to Atlanta in 1977. She was with Equifax for 25 years in a variety of roles including Senior Business Systems Analyst and Corporate Trainer. While there she earned their JV White Award for Excellence and was very active in her trade association Credit Professionals International, serving as International President in 2004 and later being named International Credit Professional of the Year.

She is a speaker, trainer, certified life coach and published author. In 2004 she started her own business, Let Your Light Shine, which now incorporates several direct sales companies, and has earned her the Kalogris Foundation Humanitarian Award .

She has been networking for over 12 years and has been leading networking groups since 2010. In 2015 she and her business partner, Tracee Randall, co-founded Atlanta Business Spotlight, which has produced multiple events such as a Financial Literacy Summit, Legacy Health Summit, Writers' Conference, and a variety of other programs and workshops, as well as a series of collaborations such as this book and last year's "The Voice That Changed Everything".

In December 2015 they started the #BeTheVoice training series which is teaching new and experienced entrepreneurs to network more effectively. Carol's green hat personality's attention to rules and detail partnered with Tracee's blue hat personality's creativity and sense of adventure have proven to be a perfect balance for a successful and innovative business model. If Tracee can envision it, Carol will find a way to make it happen.

An Xperience Connections leader for Alpharetta/Milton for over 6 years, with her business and networking expertise Carol was an obvious choice to take over as CEO of this dynamic women's empowerment organization in March 2016. At that time Atlanta Business Spotlight partnered with Bonnie Ross-Parker, who founded Xperience Connections in 2002, and Carol and Tracee are delighted to have been able to feature Bonnie and five other XC Leaders in this book.

In 2016 Carol received the Woman On Fire Merlene Samuel-Cephas Business Woman of the Year Award for Atlanta, an achievement she credits to the strong support of her Xperience Connections community.

Carol@XperienceConnections.com
www.AtlantaBusinessSpotlight.com
www.letyourlightshine.myorganogold.com
www.XperienceConnections.com
www.creditprofessionals.org
www.Facebook.com/ShineWithCarol
www.twitter.com/NCDNeal
www.LinkedIn.com/in/LetYourLightShine

See Carol's #InsiderTips on pages 59, 119, 131, 145, 161, 183, 223

Introduction

Carol D. Neal

I am so absolutely blessed in my life. I am grateful for my years in Corporate America that gave me the skills and confidence that I am able to use today in my life as an entrepreneur, but I am also grateful that I am no longer in Corporate America. Some days it is hard to imagine what my life was like before...working 60 hour weeks in an office or cubicle, my life defined JUST by work, church and family. I had no idea there was such a rich and vibrant world outside where thousands of people were waiting to meet me...people with fascinating stories and interesting products and ideas that I never knew existed. And I am SO VERY, VERY GRATEFUL that one of the first people I met in this "new" world was my business partner, Tracee Randall. It was her idea to bring some of the people we have met together to create this resource for entrepreneurs and business owners, and as always when we are walking in her #Miracle Territory, we soon realized we were on the right track!

As we began promoting the idea, the RIGHT people were attracted to the project! We began to hear from business owners who are experts in the fields of starting a business, branding, social media, networking and building a profitable multi-level marketing company. We hope that you will not take for granted the incredible tips and inspiration that are in this book. Each expert brings a new and interesting perspective and piece of the puzzle, each one is successful and has mastered their field of expertise...they are professional and profitable but willing to share their best tips with YOU! As you read the book you will notice that some of the experts touch on the same topics but just from different viewpoints. When an idea is mentioned multiple times, sit up and take notice! That means it's important, these successful experts are all using it, and that means you definitely want to follow it yourself. Success leaves clues!!!

As you read each tip, we suggest that you use this book as an on-going resource, a reference guide that you will continuously draw from. And, of course, if there is an expert that you learn something valuable from, I am going to suggest taking the following steps:

First of all, thank them! Their contact information is listed on their biography page, so send them an email sharing your testimony about what their tip did to inspire you, go to their website and share your testimony there—make yourself known to them—and then of course, put their tip into action in your own business and life!

Second, connect with them on social media and make sure you promote them and the book to others—(this is a wonderful tip you can use by the way!)—and get their attention! You might be surprised what happens when you begin to promote others who have impacted you!

Third, use their services! If they have referenced a resource that has helped them in their business, by all means it makes sense to reach out to these experts to learn more!

The following biography pages on our experts are just as important as their tips! BEFORE you begin reading the tips, I encourage you to get to know each one of our experts by reading their bio. They each have their own style and personality in addition to their unique combination of skills and experience. You will notice a strong theme in this book on the importance of people and relationships in ALL aspects of your life, not just business. Each one of our experts completely understands the power of putting relationship-building FIRST, and this is your opportunity to be mentored by and have access to some very powerful business-builders and entrepreneurs!

Enjoy, and happy connecting!

MEET THE EXPERTS

"Whoever renders service to many puts himself in line for greatness - great wealth, great return, great satisfaction, great reputation, and great joy."

~ Jim Rohn

Ires D. Alliston

Ires D. Alliston is an author, speaker and a brand strategist. She is also the Founder & CEO of the Alliston Group, LLC, a web design and internet marketing agency which received the 2015 Best of Acworth Award in the Online Marketing category. The Alliston Group offers web design, website audit, social media optimization, online reputation management, brand optimization, SEO, PPC marketing, local buzz service and video marketing.

Additionally, Ires shares her years of internet marketing experience via events, classes, workshops and webinars. She has consulted and helped numerous entrepreneurs build their business brand or professional brand, and optimize their social networks as well as address web design strategies, logo design and other online marketing topics.

To quote one of her clients, "Ires and her team were extremely professional, courteous and responsive to my needs. I had no idea of what I wanted, not even a logo. Ires and her team guided me through the process and provided me and my company with an awesome website at a very reasonable price. I highly recommend The Alliston Group for all of your website design needs" Jarrod Cody, COO of DTECINC.

Ires is available to speak at events and/or conferences with subjects related to supporting women entrepreneurs, branding strategies, business strategies and online marketing tactics. Her '1-on-1 coaching strategy' for businesses she offers also compliments her company's services. She's also an author of "Simple Branding Steps for Small Business: It Matters!" - available to download at Amazon. Furthermore, she's preparing to write her upcoming book on professional branding in the future. She's been involved and supports charitable events, work and causes as well as contributes her time with non-profit organizations. She's also a believer that when each person is moved to do good; be involved in something; however, big or small and to make a difference, a global movement of social good happens.

When she is not volunteering, she loves spending quality time with her family and friends. She's a mother of two, a former military spouse, and married for 20 plus years. Although she grew up with an entrepreneurial mother, Ires did not become an entrepreneur until much later in life as she had other pursuits growing up. She worked for various companies, completed her master's degree in business and raised her children. However, inspired by her children and husband, Duane and driven by her vision to own her online agency, she took action and launched her company in her 40's. Now she helps entrepreneurs establish their brand and presence online.

Website: www.allistongroup.com
Phone: 1-888-978-3258
Email: Info@allistongroup.com
Facebook: www.facebook.com/AllistonGroup
Google+: https://plus.google.com/+AllistonGroupLLC
LinkedIn: www.linkedin.com/in/iresalliston
Pinterest: www.pinterest.com/allistongroup
Twitter: https://twitter.com/allistongroup
YouTube: www.youtube.com/c/+AllistonGroupLLC

See Ires' #InsiderTips on pages 105, 111, 112,117, 125, 173, 179, 180, 185, 193

Taneka Badie

Taneka Badie is a native of Atlanta, Georgia. She has been an entrepreneur since the age of 15. Since a child she has always loved art and design. She earned her bachelor's of fine arts degree in graphic design from the Art Institute of Atlanta. She started her business in graphic design when she was still in college. While being an honors student she built up her clientele through resources from the school's career services department, volunteered and completed two internships. Taneka Badie is very hard working and determined to succeed in her career.

Four years later, she has expanded her business into a creative agency offering graphic design, web development, online marketing and copywriting. She manages a team and is very hands-on with every project. She is very detail oriented and that's what her clients love about her. Taneka has worked with over 100 small businesses, EMC (a Fortune 500 company), and House of Cheatham (a global hair product company). She considers herself a creative problem solver. She is an expert in branding because of her knowledge in helping brands grow from the start-up phase.

"Badie Designs not only helped develop my business, but also my brand. This company is on the cutting edge of technology and customer service. They are one of the best graphic design companies in Atlanta, GA." ~ Aubrey Geary, CEO, GearyGeorgia, LLC

Connect with Taneka:

Email: info@badiedesigns.com
Website: www.badiedesigns.com
Facebook: www.facebook.com/badiedesigns
Instagram: www.instagram.com/badiedesigns
Twitter: www.twitter.com/badiedesigns
LinkedIn: www.linkedin.com/in/tanekabadie

See Taneka's #InsiderTips on pages 67, 109, 113, 121, 177

Laura B. Baker

A wife and mother of 5, Laura uses humor and encouragement to guide those around her to see the HOPE and blessings in all of life's circumstances.

A love for educating others has enabled her to write and publish articles in trade association magazines through the years. In 2015, she was invited by the publishers to collaborate, along with 24 other authors, in the inaugural edition of the popular book series "The Voice That Changed Everything – A Book of Gratitude."

Social Media has called her into the world of video production which has led to the fulfillment of a lifelong dream of making movies. Although it is not the same as making a block buster for all to enjoy, she certainly finds it exciting to share information in this genre.

The desire to serve led Laura to jump on the opportunity to sit on the Board of Directors to the Georgia Real Estate Investors Association, Inc. In her almost 20 years of service to the Association, she has been an Officer, Director of Education, on the Ethics and Nominating Committees, and Sr. Advisor. In addition, she has also been the leader of several of the association's subgroups where the responsibilities included running the monthly meetings and arranging the topics and speakers.

Personal circumstances compelled her to take on her newest role of Wellness Advocate. After watching friends and family suffer and die from needless and preventable illnesses, she joined forces with a core group of highly regarded nutrition and wellness companies to educate people on the importance of daily habits and choices. She is a strong believer in prevention, and has personally witnessed how making a few simple changes can change a dismal outcome to a welcomed recovery.

Passionately Encouraging People to VICTORIOUS SUCCESS!

Connect with Laura:

(470) 485-HOPE (4673)
gosharehope@gmail.com
Twitter: @laurabbaker
FaceBook: /laurabbaker.mindset

See Laura's #InsiderTips on pages 139, 149, 155, 159, 189

Dannella Burnett

Beginning with a love of food and with Julia Child as an inspiration, Dannella has worked in the culinary and special events field since the age of 16. She has degrees in Culinary Arts and Food Service Management from Johnson and Wales University. Among other awards, she earned Gold Medals in both London and Germany for International Culinary Competitions.

Following college, she managed restaurants, catered and coordinated events and weddings in Washington DC and Virginia, always bridging the gap between vision and execution. Dannella moved to Georgia to be closer to family in 2001. In 2009, when her husband lost his job in the construction field, Dannella created Oakwood Occasions to provide North Georgia with quality event solutions and to support her family. "Necessity may be the Mother of Invention, but Mothers are Inventive by Necessity" says Dannella. Over the years Oakwood Occasions has offered custom catering, high-end vending options, OO Fudge shipped nationally, coffee services with Organo Coffee, OO Coffee Shoppe, OO Café and event management and wedding coordination.

She's been featured in several publications and won awards across North Georgia. Named 2 years in a row in Gwinnett Magazine's People to Know and Best Event Planner in North Georgia 2016. Dannella also has a heart for serving others and her location has been an intern site for Project Success for 4 years serving Special Needs Young Adults and she was just selected a Power Of the Purse Community Hero for the launch of Project RePurse serving women in recovery and transitioning from domestic violence or other difficulties. She is a leader for the South Hall, Georgia, Xperience Connections.

Now an author and sought after speaker for women's empowerment, small business ownership and event solutions, Dannella is truly a creative entrepreneur that believes in multiple streams of income and always finding the Win-Win-Win combination. Through creative partnerships with her incredible network as well as high level of experience, Dannella brings everything to the table needed to make your event a success!

Connect with Dannella:

www.facebook.com/DannellaMcWilliamsBurnett
www.Facebook.com/OakwoodOccasions
www.Facebook.com/DannellaBurnett.OrganoGold
www.Twitter.com/OakwoodOccasion
www.LinkedIn.com/in/DannellaBurnett
www.OakwoodOccasions.com
www.OakwoodOccasions.OrganoGold.com
Office 770-297-4750
Cell 678-677-3858

See Dannella's #InsiderTips on pages 47, 69, 77, 83, 95, 209, 225

Carole Cheatam

Business Strategist/Life and Wellness Coach/Entrepreneur

With 50+ years of experience, Carole Cheatam is committed to help others tap into their inherent gifts and rediscover their purpose through business.

A native of New Jersey, she attended undergraduate and law school at Rutgers University. With the thought of temporarily putting her law career on hold, she became a stay-at-home Mom; it was then the entrepreneurial flame was fanned. She ran several successful traditional businesses centered around her talent as an artist.

Several years ago, Carole was enticed out of "retirement" by a health and wellness company in the direct sales industry. Besides the ability to make a substantial income, it has afforded her the opportunity to travel, network, and teach others to be successful. Taking charge of her own health, she changed her eating habits and started to exercise regularly and is now an avid runner, competing in her first race at 65! As a health and life coach she has recently founded Rediscovering You where she coaches individuals to use their gifts and talents to start their own businesses and helps them commit to make their health a priority through healthy eating and exercise.

Carole is the Xperience Connections leader for Lawrenceville/Grayson, Georgia.

Her favorite personal quote is: "You're never too old to learn something new from anyone."

Connect with Carole:

Email: ccheatam@gmail.com
Website: www.Re-Discovering-You.com

See Carole's #InsiderTips on pages 199, 205, 213, 219, 220, 231

Xperience
connections
Women Make It Happen!

Stephanie Combes

Stephanie Combes is an inventor, entrepreneur and event planner who has taken the Atlanta market by storm with her incredible mobile phone-charging power bank, Instatricity. She has a huge heart for non-profits and recently combined her very successful Instatricity fundraiser program with the NextSteps Youth Entrepreneur Program, securing the position of Network Service Agency for the thriving non-profit. She is an avid networker and an accomplished speaker.

Stephanie has proven that being an entrepreneur takes persistence and commitment, and she has done it in conjunction with home-schooling her 3 amazing children, ages 8, 10, and 17. She and her husband are teaming together to create a legacy not just for their own children, but for other young and aspiring entrepreneurs as well. The question that constantly leaves her lips is "What can I do for you?" and she understands that servant leadership is the highest form.

This self-proclaimed "Obstacle Mover" has a creative mind, always thinking of and executing ways she can partner with other businesses and organizations—putting the needs of other small business owners first, and in so doing creating trusting and valuable relationships globally.

Within months of entering the Atlanta market, Stephanie became known as the "woman to know", and through her incredible networking skills she has been sought after to be a part of major events and collaborations. She is the Xperience Connections leader for the North Gwinnett, Georgia area, empowering and supporting women in business. She was recently one of the sponsors at a regional quarterly women's event, EntrepreNewHER where she held the audience enamored with her incredibly funny and entertaining style—relating to the audience with her candid and transparent fun-loving humor!

Stephanie is a powerful source and resource—above all she is sincere, consistent and persistent in achieving her goals and helping and equipping others achieve theirs!

Connect with Stephanie:

www.Facebook.com/instatricity
www.Twitter.com/instatricity
Email: awesome@instatricity.com
Website: www.instatricity.com

See Stephanie's #InsiderTips on pages 50, 54, 60, 75, 93, 147

Deborah Daniel, CPA

Deborah Daniel, Founder of Charter Accounting, became an entrepreneur in 1993 soon after completing her MBA. During the last 23 years she has purchased and scaled four smaller accounting firms to achieve a client base of over 1,000 annual recurring clients. During this time she and her husband have owned and sold several other companies both on their own and with partners for total values in excess of ten million dollars. In addition to operating businesses, she has extensive knowledge and ownership in real estate investment and uses this hands-on knowledge to mentor clients in the areas of tax planning, investment planning and financial and wealth creation habits and strategies. By helping clients figure out what numbers *really matter* in their business and showing them how to measure and evaluate these key indicators, she helps business owners take their businesses to the next level.

In addition, Deborah leads the Atlanta Chapter of eWomenNetwork, Inc. which is widely recognized as the Premier Women's Business Network in North America. In her leadership role, she has developed networking strategies that have grown her business as well as the businesses of her members.

Deborah speaks and blogs on the topics of entrepreneurship, wealth creation, women in business and networking. She and her husband of 24 years, Edward, have a teenage son and daughter and are active in several organizations in the Northern Atlanta suburbs.

Connect with Deborah:

Twitter @deborahdcpa
Facebook https://www.facebook.com/deborahdanielcpa
Deborah@charteraccounting.com
770-671-0021

See Deborah's #InsiderTips on pages 45, 55, 63, 73, 79, 89, 141, 148, 157

Susan Guthrie

Susan has been in the Wellness and Network Marketing industries for over 16 years. Her passion is in educating people on safe natural ways to improve their health. She does that by encouraging them to make small changes daily that improve their quality of life forever. Susan is a Nutritional Cleanse coach with Isagenix. She has mentored her team of Consultants to successfully coach many people to release weight, improve their health and build residual income. She coached a winner of the IsaBody Challenge who released over 150 pounds and won $5,000 in a National Contest.

Susan is married and has two grown children who all share the Isagenix products and income. They have all improved their health releasing over 150 pounds as a family.

She enjoys volunteering with many organizations. Her philosophy is "A lot of people doing a little bit can make a big difference in the lives of others".

Susan is the President of the Cobb Business Women's Association where she leads Community Service projects each month. She is also the leader of the Powder Springs Xperience Connections where she enjoys hosting and connecting women in business.

Susan graduated from the University of Georgia with a BS in Horticulture and taught High School Horticulture for 8 years. She has been a Florist for over 32 years and currently owns Florals to Remember, specializing in weddings.

Connect with Susan:

404-402-9168
wellnessnetwork@comcast.net
www.wellnessnetwork.biz

See Susan's #InsiderTips on pages 201, 207, 215, 227, 233

Angela Hemans

Brand and Marketing Strategist, Social Media Trainer

Angela holds a bachelor's degree in Business Administration from Saint Leo University. Her background includes helping patients as a cardiovascular sonographer, but her passion for entrepreneurs and entrepreneurship has led her to diagnostics of a different sort.

Angela founded the Women United in Business Association to facilitate networking, promoting, and experience-sharing among women business owners.

She enjoys working with business professionals and authors from diverse industries and backgrounds to develop and implement tailored sales solutions. To this end, she helps small business owners establish an online presence, or platform, that enhances their brand through social media and marketing communications, and helps business owners improve social media and networking skills.

Because it's much easier to create products and service than it is to sell them, Angela's insight and know-how helps small business owners establish themselves in their industry and attract a fan base that will not only buy from them but will value what they offer and therefore are able to inspire and make an impact on others.

For more resources on branding, Twitter marketing, and social media help, Angela can be contacted on her website.

Connect with Angela:

www.AngelaHemans.com
Email: Angela@AngelaHemans.com
Twitter: wwww.twitter.com/angelahemans
Facebook: www.facebook.com/TheAngelaHemans

See Angela's #InsiderTips on pages 107, 175, 181, 187, 191, 195

Jody P. Humphrey

Jody P. Humphrey is a National Field Director for Hegemon Group International. A Georgia native, Jody attended Brigham Young University, where he studied Business.

Specialized Experience

Jody has had a front row seat to the greatest marketing movement in the history of financial services. He has developed a unique leadership style by studying and emulating the great leaders he has had the opportunity to work with both personally and professionally. Chief among his mentors is his father Hubert Humphrey, an industry icon. Jody followed in Hubert's footsteps by working in the marketing and team building side of financial services distribution. Over his 20+ year career Jody has built his own legacy of success by building and developing over 400+ $100,000 earners. He has earned numerous industry awards including the prestigious "Leader of the Year" in 2007-2008.

Business Affiliations
-National Sales Director, A.L. Williams 1984-1990
-Executive Field Chairman, World Marketing Alliance 1990-2001
-Senior Marketing Director, World Leadership Group 2001-2008
-Owner JPH Marketing Systems, 2008-current

Key Projects

1-Vice President of Marketing and Sales, KBR Capital Partners 2008-2011

2-Director of Sales, Training and Business Development, Vida Cup International 2012-2014

3-National Field Director, Hegemon Group International 2014-present

Personal and Professional Awards and Affiliations

-Served a mission for The Church of Jesus Christ of Latter Day Saints

-Member of Who's Who of America

-Voting member of the Country Music Association

-Recognized by Congress as an "Angel of Adoption" for work in adoption development

-Eagle Scout in the Boys Scouts of America organization

Connect with Jody:

JPHMarketingSystems@gmail.com

See Jody's #InsiderTips on pages 210, 221

JoBeth Martin

For as long as she can remember JoBeth's desire has been to have a life changing impact on the lives of those around her. She and her husband Doug have been married 35 years. They have five amazing daughters, three sons-in-law so far and four beautiful grandchildren. After completing degrees from Columbia International University in Bible and Berry College in Secondary Education she spent 4 years as a classroom teacher.

The birth of her first child began a season of 28 years as a full time mom and homeschool educator. For 10 years she served on the Board of Directors of CFE and CHAT Educational Support Groups. She has participated as a leader and teacher in numerous women's Bible Studies and as an organizer and speaker at Women's Retreats.

The mission of JoBeth's company, "Righteous Oaks," is to empower women to be all that they were created to be in every area of life; personal, family, relational and business. As an entrepreneur, JoBeth presently represents two companies, Nerium International and Ruby Ribbon; supporting women to live confidently in their individual beauty. She also freelances as a Floral Designer.

She especially loves to inspire and mentor women one on one, in small groups and as a speaker to larger women's groups. Her gifting is to communicate clearly the deeper truths of life, to identify the lies that hold us back and encourage individuals to walk in the truth of their God given creation.

She is a leader with Xperience Connections Kennesaw/Town Center in Georgia.

Connect with JoBeth:

Jobeth.martin@outlook.com
(770) 845-1821
http://HisRighteousOaks.com
www.jobethm.nerium.com
www.rubyribbon.com/jobethmartin
www.facebook.com/jobeth.p.martin

See JoBeth's #InsiderTips on pages 61, 87, 115, 123, 151, 211, 229

Corey 'NetworKing' Moore

Corey Moore has provided targeted strategies and financial consulting to small business owners for more than ten years. He is passionate about equipping clients with the knowledge and tools that promote business growth. Through his company, Fortune Financial Group, Corey creates strategies for effective and efficient budgets, lowering tax liabilities, and increasing business revenue.

Corey's second passion encompasses helping entrepreneurs and sales associates promote their brand through networking. Corey created ProNetworker, LLC, a resource center where sales professionals can find networking events around Atlanta. ProNetworker teaches that while at these business events, professionals should be networking to find the three C's; A Client, A Collaborator, and/or A Competitor. ProNetworker goes a step further by also producing networking events, workshops, business expos, and more. Corey has also produced events that featured celebrities like Daymond John and Kevin Harrington, both stars of ABC's 'Shark Tank'. Corey attributes all of his success from networking. He is a firm believer that it is not what you know, nor who you know, but who knows you that matters.

Connect with Corey:

Fortune Financial Group, LLC
Website – www.ffgga.com
Phone – 678.921.2929
Email – cmoore@ffgga.com

ProNetworker, LLC
Website – www.ProNetworker.com
Phone – 404.594.1494
Email – corey@pronetworker.com

See Corey's #InsiderTips on pages 51, 65, 81, 91, 143

Bonnie Ross-Parker

In August of 2002, Bonnie created The Joy of Connecting®, dba Xperience Connections™, a program supporting professional women nationwide. After having over 4,000 women in her home and reaching thousands of women nationwide, Xperience Connections™ continues its growth in collaboration with Atlanta Business Spotlight LLC.

Bonnie is the author of several books including *Walk In My Boots: The Joy of Connecting*, shifting your consciousness to share yourself with others and *Y.O.U. ~ Set A High Standard for Being Human* showing how our journey impacts others and the journey of others impacts our own.

She is also a contributing author to *What We Talk About When We're Over Sixty* by Sherri Davis and Linda Hughes and *Atlanta's Real Women* by Linda Hughes and Christine Martinello and several others where she describes how a mother copes with the loss of a child.

Her most recent book, *Discovery and Recovery: A Shared Journey* chronicles her 8-month challenge with Breast Cancer taking the reader through the entire process from diagnoses through chemo, surgery, radiation and recovery. It is available on-line at no charge.

www.bonnierossparker.com/discovery-and-recovery/download.php

Bonnie has received numerous awards, among them, the Athena International Award Program and the Toastmaster's International Communication and Leadership Award, and she was also recognized as a Georgia woman of influence by The Woman's Leadership Exchange of New York.

In May, 2010, Bonnie was recognized as a distinguished business woman – part of the Princess Diana Tour/Atlanta. In November, 2014 Bonnie was acknowledged by *PointsNorth Atlanta Magazine* as being 1 of 11 recipients to be featured in their cover story: *"Savvy & Successful – Our Annual Tribute to Local Inspiring Women"* In December, 2014, The Atlanta Business & Entertainment Exchange presented her with the "Leadership Award" with the inscription: "Thank you for your commitment and dedication to the Atlanta Community".

While she has faced and overcome many challenges, Bonnie Ross-Parker has never lost her focus and enthusiasm for life. She believes that the possibilities are endless for those who value and nurture relationships.

Bonnie is a working example of what is possible when we focus, take action and chart our own course. She has spent her entire life encouraging women to do just that. She continues to be a tireless mentor of women helping them to maximize collaborative vs. competitive relationships.

"Connection is not some topic Bonnie decided to write about...it's her way of life!" *Susan RoAnn, Best selling author of How To Work*

Connect with Bonnie:

770-333-7923
brossparker@gmail.com
www.BonnieRossParker.com

See Bonnie's #InsiderTips on pages 133, 135, 137, 163, 165, 167

Mark A. Sterling

Mark A. Sterling is a leadership catalyst whose expertise equips emerging leaders with tips, tools and techniques to realize their full potential. Prior to entering the direct sales industry, Mark was an IT consultant providing services for Fortune 500 companies and government entities as well as International clients. During Mark's dozen plus years of direct sales experience, he has worked with some of the industry's top leaders.

In his current project, Mark has assisted more than 10 team members in his network achieve six-figure incomes. He has grown organizations that have spanned dozens of countries and has trained on multiple continents. He is a principled leader who abides by the hierarchy of faith, family and then finances. His immediate goal is to assist 100 families in creating six-figure residual annual incomes. He strongly believes that through FAITH, hard work and persistence, ALL things are possible.

Favorite Quote: "You must be able to see your goals behind your eyes, so that you can see them in front of your eyes!"

Connect with Mark: sterling@sterlinglife.biz

See Mark's #InsiderTips on pages 49, 53, 56, 80, 99, 217

TIPS ON
STARTING AND RUNNING
A BUSINESS

"Sweat equity is the most valuable equity there is.
Know your business and industry better than anyone
else in the world.
Love what you do or don't do it."

~Mark Cuban

Measure What Counts!

Deborah Daniel

If you don't have a destination in mind, no matter how far you travel you will never get there! This is true in life and definitely in business. It is never all about the money but unless you are gaining a lot of quality of life benefits owning a business you had better be making more than you can in the 9-5 world or it is time to shine up the resume! I have been consulting with small business owners and self- employed professionals for just shy of a quarter century and I have seen far too many of them working 90 hours a week for themselves to avoid working 40 hours for someone else—but making far less than they would have as an employee. The sad part is most of them had the skills to succeed in business— just not the information to see what they were missing.

In most businesses the information is there—you just have to know where to look for it. Unfortunately many entrepreneurs use what I call the checkbook method of measuring their success. This method means if there is money in the checkbook—the business is doing well! That cannot be further from the truth—there are other way more important numbers. Even though I am a CPA and look at Profit and Loss statements and Balance Sheets constantly to help my clients with their taxes and business, these are not the numbers I mean when I say measure what counts.

How much is an average customer worth to you? What is your retention level if you have recurring revenue or your repeat sales by customer? What is your close rate on sales conversations? These kinds of performance indicators are the kinds of numbers I think you need to measure to gauge where the business is. For example if you want to add $10,000 in revenue—and your average customer spends $400—that means you need 25 new sales. If you have to offer your service three times to get a yes (that means a 33% closing rate), you must have 75 sales conversations to add the desired $10,000. From here you would have to come up with a strategy of how to have those 75 conversations. But without this info you will get discouraged when the $10,000 doesn't come after you only talked to 10 people!!

Every business is different so there are no standards for what numbers need to be measured in a company. I am very competitive and without any real performance measure given to me by my boss (that's ME!) I came up with my own measurement system. A major source of revenue in our business is tax returns so I set up a spreadsheet that keeps up with numbers of returns completed by the firm per day and season to date and this sheet compares the season to date to the last three years. I watch these numbers daily to gauge if we are on track to meet or beat the past three years' performance, and if we fall behind I have the information to determine if course corrections are needed. I don't track the revenue by day, just the total number of returns, because if the activity is happening I know (based on the numbers I have been tracking) that the revenue is also there!

Sometimes you need to slow down in your business in order to speed up. Slow down, take a hard look at your business, and come up with a few key numbers you need to track to keep a better handle on your business performance. I promise you—your bottom line will appreciate it!

Strategic Partnerships and Alliances

Dannella Burnett

Let's face it, we can't do it alone!! As an event planner I see firsthand that it takes a village to create an event, a product roll-out, or to fulfill the needs of your clients. We often get into the trap of trying to do it all ourselves and may end up frustrated, overworked or worse, not meeting the needs of our clients. Look at your vendors and your contacts and see if there is a great match for sharing your clients or sharing the work load. This allows you to be more efficient, more focused and hopefully put more money into your pocket by exposing your business to your Strategic Partner's Client base as well!

Let me give an example. We have a client, a pretty major national client that has a local operation with over 500 employees. We have the privilege of producing their annual employee event. It's a day long affair with food, entertainment, gifts for the employees and their families...all in all we plan for 1500 guests and oversee every aspect of this event. We COULD do it all, but this is a major project!! Far better to bring in vendors that do all these elements especially well and create an experience for the guests that is memorable and executable. We partner with our favorite rental company, entertainment company, AV company and even though we can cater events for 1500 ourselves, we partnered with a local catering company and gave them the opportunity to show off their amazing food. All in all our client only dealt with one vendor but we coordinated the efforts of 8 different vendors to produce the event to match our client's vision and budget. That's partnering that works!

Another example is the product of another author in this book, *Instatricity* with Stephanie Combes. As soon as I saw this product I knew there was a strategic partnership in the works. It's a powerful portable phone charger. At many of the events we coordinate there is a need for vendors and attendees to charge their phones. We can partner with Instatricity, give them the platform to showcase their products and services and we save the event money by not having to rent charging stations or paying additional electrical fees to venues. It's a win-win-win, just the way we like it!

Get creative, as you network and meet with new contacts, think about your target audience, your current clients and the markets you would like to tap into. Do you and your contacts share that audience? Can you join forces in a way that is mutually beneficial? Can you combine resources or products and create a new joint package or promotion? Can you save money or reach a larger audience by working together? These types of partnerships, strategic and defined, can really help you advance your company and save the bottom line!

What You See is What You Get

Mark A. Sterling

Often times we have heard that 'I need to see it in order to believe it,' but they are referring to the physical manifestation of the thing.

Visualization will allow you to go there (goals, desired results) before you get there. For instance, Natan Sharansky, a computer specialist who spent 9 years in prison in the USSR after being accused of spying for the U.S., masterfully leveraged the principles of visualization. While in solitary confinement, he played himself in mental chess, saying: "I might as well use the opportunity to become the world champion!" Remarkably, in 1996, Sharansky beat world champion chess player Garry Kasparov! Seeing your goals and dreams in the present allows you to create the future that you desire.

I remember creating vision boards when I first began my walk down the personal development and entrepreneur path. It definitely helped me but I wanted to accelerate my results, so I DECIDED (that's a powerful word) to start creating VISION ENVIRONMENTS! I challenge you to create a vision environment. Have pictures of your desired state everywhere that you frequent. Your future is bigger than a board.

I had images of my family, finances, travel destinations and future possessions in every room of my home, in my car and in my wallet.

I had written affirmations on my bathroom mirror, above light switches throughout my home, on the ceiling above my bed. I know that one sounds a tad obsessive and out of the ordinary but I NEEDED extra-ordinary results and what better way than to see my future as soon as I opened my eyes?

"You must see it behind your eyes, so that you can see it before your eyes."   ~ Mark A. Sterling

People are Lonely Because They Build Walls Not Bridges

Stephanie Combes

And so it goes for business as well. Being an entrepreneur is no easy task. It involves taking an idea or a dream and turning it into a reality. Dreams have to include other people. Dreams that take place in an open meadow of solitude are happy ones to be sure, but the ones that include dialogue stick in our minds the most. We tend to build walls instead of bridges in our hearts and it trickles down into our business minds. We hear that there is more strength in unity, and small businesses need to lean on the shoulders of their neighbors in order to thrive. The question, "What can I do for you?" should always be in your mind as an entrepreneur.

I once mentored the owner of a local flower shop that was within short range of a retirement community. I worked to create a bond between the two seemingly different organizations and added to the range of goods that were offered. This gave new light to an older community and added new heart to the otherwise common flower shop. People want to have relationships with other people. Companies want to have relationships with other companies. The retirement home created an additional stream of income for the residents and the flower shop received a tremendous amount of PR, press and accolades. There was even a community cleanup day dedicated to a makeover of the flower shop and a beautiful grand re-opening to feature the collaboration of these two small businesses.

Collaborating opens doors to more revenue. No matter how small a business, they have something to offer a bigger business and vice versa. In order to be a successful entrepreneur, you should visualize your surroundings as an extension of your own brand. If a store is in the middle of nowhere, with no other business around them, they may not gain as much foot traffic. It's when businesses are laced together and supporting one another, that the money begins to flow. Always network, and always be creatively available. Opportunity is always knocking!

The 'B' is Good

Corey Moore

Question: How can a person expect to be able to budget $100,000 if they can't budget $100?

When starting a business, one of the most important things to master is the art of budgeting your money. Regardless of how great your product or service is, how good your marketing is, even if your sales continue to increase; if you can't budget your money effectively, you will surely go out of business.

First: Do a budget for your personal finances. Even though you may not be happy with your current financial situation, it is extremely important to know how much it costs you to live each month.

Second: Once you have calculated your monthly living expenses, try to work diligently to lower that number by cutting expenses. No one likes cutting anything out of their life but consider the big picture: every dollar not spent on a personal expense can be invested into growing your business.

Third: Do a budget for your business. You need to know exactly how much it takes for you to operate your business every month.

Fourth: Try to lower that number. The number one way to increase revenue is to lower expenses. See if you can make the same amount of sales while spending less money.

Note: You should keep your personal finances and your business finances completely separate from one another. The reason is, worst case scenario, if one of them runs out of money, the other will survive. If they are combined, when one sinks, they both sink.

Always know exactly how much it costs you to live in a month and how much it costs you to operate your business. Take those two numbers and add them together. Then take the amount you would profit if you made one sale. Take the profit number and divide it into the total of the two numbers you added together. This will let you know how many sales you need every month to ensure all bills get paid. You now have the start to a 'Sales Goal'.

It's OK to Fail

Mark A. Sterling

It's OK to fail. Just fail quickly. Success is not final, nor is failure fatal. Failing is merely the universe's way of providing course correction. Mistakes are the GPS for wisdom.

We can avoid some mistakes by having mentors and/or following successful paths that have already been traveled but often times we get greater revelation from the personal experience of failure. I remember my mother and aunts telling me when I was growing up that a hard head makes for a soft behind. Translation: Sometimes we must fail in spite of being given good counsel. The experience becomes more personal and more real.

If you think trying is expensive, just wait until you get the bill for doing nothing.

Utilize All Your Space and Abilities

Stephanie Combes

I have always believed that small businesses hold the key to true success. However, they may not always see the potential themselves. I have worked around the clock and around different locations to get my name out there as a loyal contact to many small businesses in the Denver and Atlanta areas. I strive to give new light and encourage small businesses, startups, and up and coming programs to use every aspect of their business to build revenue. By building partnerships and always looking for the next connection to be made, abundance is easier to achieve.

I was first introduced to this idea when I stepped into a marketing role at a small bakery. The foundation was there, the creative expansion had yet to be noticed. The bakery offered delivery of the goods as a very congenial service. However, an even better use of time and transport would be offering catering. I canvassed the busy tech area and found there was more than enough business to go around. Within weeks, we transformed part of the kitchen and the extra room in the back of the facility to be used as a rented meeting space, and a small office for bride consultations. When all space and all resources are used, production is more efficient.

I knew I needed a personal assistant to free up some of my non-productive time. Time is precious and I needed to release about 10 hours a week. I didn't know that my budget would support it right away so I had to look for more creative ways to sweeten the pot. I had a spare room in my house that I offered in exchange for someone helping me for 40 hours a month. Not only did that free up some of my time to spend with my family, but it offered me the additional time to generate another stream of income.

Leave no stone unturned, no shelf empty, no room unmanaged, and no talent underutilized!

Being in Business FOR Yourself Doesn't Mean BY Yourself!

Deborah Daniel

Most successful entrepreneurs are fairly independent souls— I think it is part of the job description. But the really successful entrepreneurs are the ones who know when they need to ask for help—and ask for it! Early in the startup phase it is important to assemble key advisors that will partner with you in your business. This "dream team" is made up of the pieces of expertise that you as the business owner don't already have. Every business needs a banker, a lawyer and a financial advisor at a minimum. You need to establish these relationships before you need to call on them. You want your banker to know you before you need them to know you. Going to a bank to seek a line of credit for a big order will be a lot easier if you already have that relationship!

You got into business because the product or service you have adds value to your customers and your role is to present and enhance that value. While you may have some knowledge on all parts of your business – you can't be an expert on everything and you shouldn't try. In addition to these outside advisors you need to bring in internal resources to fill gaps in your skills set right away as well. Even before you are ready for employees you can get help by outsourcing tasks. A virtual assistant and social media expert are two examples of team members that will free up time for you to do the tasks only YOU can do. I am fairly active on Social Media, but having someone help me with content and strategy enables me to focus on areas of the business where I have more expertise.

Many issues in your business you can handle yourself—but just because you can do everything in your business definitely does not mean you should. I would challenge you to surround yourself with the right "dream team" team to smooth the path to a more profitable business.

STOP Making New Year's Resolutions!

Mark A. Sterling

Every new year people make many "New Year's Resolutions". The two most popular ones are:
1. Lose weight
2. Make more money

The simple disciplines of losing weight and making more money often fade within the first few days. The crowded gyms are nearly empty by mid-January and the thoughts of making more money diminish and are relegated to next year.

STOP making resolutions. Instead make DECISIONS.

Where you are is NOT who you are. Where you are now is often a result of your past decisions. Your future is shaped by the decisions you are making right NOW.

Harness the Power of Our Decisions

Understanding the root of the word DECISION is helpful.
DE – out of, and CISION – to cut

We must cut something out of our lives that no longer serves us in order to make room for those things that will.

Fortify your decision with a commitment

Now make an unshakeable decision to follow through on your decision. Begin taking immediate action. Free yourself mentally by knowing that your decision may not be perfect when you make it. That is OK. We can always make adjustments. We can always make a decision "more right" later. You don't need to know every detail of the process before you begin.

They Just Don't "Think"

Tracee Randall

Most of us have at least heard about Robert Kiyosaki and his book, <u>Rich Dad, Poor Dad</u>. In it, he writes about the "Rich and Wealthy" vs the "Poor and Middle Class". Recently one of my mentors taught me that there is really only one major difference between the "R&W" and the "P&MC"-- it's the way they THINK. Claude Bristol, in his book, <u>The Magic of Believing</u> says it this way, "Most men (or women—my 'add') just don't THINK."

The most important tip I can give a small business owner, an entrepreneur, a stay-at-home mom, a high school or college student, an artist, a mechanic, or someone who is considering STARTING A BUSINESS.........change the way you *THINK*.....and if you aren't already "thinking", then start!

I have always been more positive than negative, always seeing the cup 1/2 full instead of 1/2 empty---but in 2015 I made it a point to change this area of my life....to *in fact*, <u>Think and Grow Rich</u> (another incredible book by Napoleon Hill). I purposed to *listen* to a book on CD every single day without fail, no excuses. I listened in the morning as I was getting dressed. I listened in my car on the drive to a meeting, I listened at my computer, I listened at night as I went to sleep. I didn't miss a day or an opportunity, and most of the books I listened to not once, but multiple times. It was that year that *EVERYTHING* dramatically changed for me personally and in my business. My business exploded. I can honestly say that making this a daily practice (which becomes a habit) has been instrumental in doubling and now tripling my income. Now that I have created this habit it is a daily part of my life. For me, it's like taking a bath or brushing my teeth—non-negotiable.

The books that have impacted me the most as far as mindset and changing the way I think are the three mentioned above and the following: <u>The Strangest Secret</u> by Earl Nightingale, and <u>The Science of Getting Rich</u> by Wallace D. Wattles. I would like to make mention here too that reading is amazing, I am an avid reader, always have been, BUT—there is something about LISTENING to a book in addition to reading it. HEARING it is important, so don't miss that point!

I suggest purchasing the CD of the works or downloading them onto a device—most are available for free on YouTube. Listening is best because you can listen while driving, sleeping, getting dressed and while moving around. Doing housework and mundane activity while listening to these incredible works will take you and your business to a whole new level! One of my mentors would always say to me, "Success leaves clues." Who are the rich and wealthy? Who are the successful entrepreneurs and business tycoons? Who are the self-made millionaires? Identify them and then DO WHAT THEY DO. I was amazed when I found out that Oprah Winfrey has read the book <u>Think and Grow Rich</u> over 13 times! Whether you agree with him or not, Donald Trump has attributed much of his success on the principles in this book—Warren Buffet quotes it as well. For me, this book has been second only to the Bible in its impact on my life, and frankly, one reading is just not enough!

Another incredible resource is a movie titled "The Secret" by Rhonda Byrne. I do want to point out that I am a Christian. I am not "religious" (big difference!) but there are things in all of these works that don't "sit right" with my faith. I didn't allow that to stop me from learning from them. I combined and wrapped my faith and spiritual beliefs around the principles that they taught and even became stronger in my faith and relationship with God because of it. God gave me an idea for a workshop titled "Make Up Your Mind" as a result of my search for mind power. Don't allow that to be your excuse for not listening.

Start today. No excuses. This tip will rock your world!

Learning to SHINE

Carol D. Neal

Elsewhere in this book I talk about my own brand, Let Your Light Shine. I have also used SHINE as an acronym to remind myself of some important tips for success that, if implemented, will help you #BeTheVoice that stands out in the crowd.

Serve – put others first. Always enter a new relationship with the goal in mind of determining what you can do for the other person, not the other way around. Volunteer (see Laura Baker's tips on this) Be the "go to" person, the person that people know will be able to find them the perfect resource, the best referral. Give freely with no expectation of receiving but rest comfortably in the knowledge that you WILL receive when you embrace the servant leadership mindset.

Hone – hone your skills, sharpen the axe. Practice, practice, practice your people and presentation skills. Push yourself to strengthen your weaknesses. Read or listen to self-development every day. Take classes. Find a mentor and an accountability partner. Ask your team members, up, down and cross-line, for feedback. Be vulnerable enough to get other people's viewpoints and be willing to implement their suggestions.

Innovate – you need to come up with new and creative solutions to stand out from the crowd. Think outside the box when meeting your clients' needs or streamlining your own processes. Stay on top of new technology and new ideas.

Nurture – mentor others, build relationships, follow-up and follow-through on your promises, and don't forget to take care of yourself, too (follow Tracee Randall's tip on this)!

Edify – there is great power in learning to PROPERLY edify and promote others. The star that shines the brightest is the one that shines its light on others!

Shoot Now, Aim Later

Stephanie Combes

It is important to have a plan for your business. It is easier to kick start your product when you know where to start. However, this world is ever changing. Demand is ever changing. The trick to this is always being open to changing that plan. Too many companies have lost their momentum because they are so set in their own ways. Just because something worked 30 years ago, 1 year ago, or even last week, doesn't mean it will work today. Always be ready to change. Always make innovation part of your plan.

Look at the phone in your hand. How long have you had it? My guess is, probably no longer than 1 or 2 years. That is because technology is always coming out with the "next best thing." Stay on your toes and keep your head in the clouds. Marketing, structure, and business plans can change at the drop of a hat. Goals are important but risks pack just as strong of a punch.

My main issue with small business owners is that they are all ideas and plans, but no action. I am not asking you to discount your original plan or your original goals. They are what have gotten you to where you are now and have given you the motivation to even read this book of tips. I am asking you to never cap out, never set limits. Channel the youth inside of yourself and follow that inspiration, but don't be afraid of something outside of your comfort zone and your business plan. Shoot now, aim later.

Grow Before You Think You Need To

JoBeth Martin

What an interesting title, "Grow Before You Think You Need To." Does it make sense? From experience I can say yes!

We need to maximize our strengths and work on our weaknesses. We know as entrepreneurs that much of our success in business depends on what we bring to the table. When you own your own business the buck stops here. Willingness to work as hard on yourself as you do on your business can mean the difference between success and failure. You either grow or die in this world.

We have all seen leaders who seem to succeed effortlessly. If we compare ourselves with these successful individuals we can come to the false belief that if I just want it badly enough, I will be like them and succeed also. What we may not be seeing is that they have been through years of personal growth to get where they are today. Their previous growth prepared them for today.

So why the title, "Grow Before You Think You Need To?" There is wisdom in taking inventory of our strengths and weaknesses. Once you have a good picture, then make a plan to grow in your area of weakness or make provision for another way of meeting those needs. Here's a quick story to illustrate my point.

In my present MLM, Nerium International, I had quick success. I reached all the initial goals and my organization and business grew quickly. It seemed easy. What I was not aware of at the time is that the initial activities needed for success totally played into my strengths. I am a communicator and a relationship person. Those skills worked well for the initial building phases of my business. However, eventually my organization became bigger than what I could manage with my personal skills and I hit the wall. My lack of organizational skills showed up.

If I had known that I needed to grow in that area, or at the very least find team members who were strong and delegate it to them, I would not have hit that wall. I would have already grown into the need. You don't have to take years preparing to start; simply be aware and honest about your strengths and make a plan for your weaknesses.

What have I learned? To admit when I need help. I am proactive to learn and grow even when it is difficult and before I get in totally over my head. The good thing is that even failure brings growth and we can do it better in the future. I recently became a leader with a Women's Networking group called Xperience Connections. I love to lead, to network, to speak and build relationships. But remember, I do have a weakness in the area of organization. So I found a partner, Arlene Cohen, who is truly my better half. She is a CPA and is meticulous with the details. Where I would wing it and go with the flow, she knows all the rules and keeps us in line. I encourage her to function in her strengths and I am learning from her. I am not afraid to say that I don't know how to do something and ask for her help. Maybe I would have struggled less in the past if I had been willing to ask for help sooner. It's a great partnership. We laughingly say, I'll do the talking and she can do the rest. Arlene knows I'm not letting her off the hook that easily. She will get chances to talk and grow in that area too. Don't be too nervous Arlene; after all, what are partners for?

Don't Be a One Trick Pony!

Deborah Daniel

Diversification is a strategy that many wealth advisors promote for financial security. I agree and I also believe revenue diversification is key to business success and longevity. By business diversification I mean some form of multiple streams or sources of income.

There are four main ways that you can earn income. The first and probably the most common is trading dollars for hours either in a job in the corporate world or in your own business when what you charge is based on the time you spend. In this revenue model you don't make money when you take time off! This is the way most professional services such as accountants and lawyers charge—the fee is based on an hourly rate and how much time is spent.

The second revenue model involves leveraging your time. This type of revenue has pricing that is not based on just the time spent. Examples of this would be project pricing or value pricing which bases pricing on the completed project or value received and steps away from the direct relationship between the time spent and the revenue received. An example of this would be instead of charging a client to go to their office and set up QuickBooks, I can have a seminar that 10 people attend and learn the setup and I can duplicate it multiple times.

Recurring revenue is the third possible stream of income in your arsenal. This can be any form of residual income whether it is from building a direct sales team in any of the hundreds of multi-level marketing businesses, creating a membership program, licensing your intellectual property to others, earning royalties from a book, movie or song, or even earning rent from a property you own and lease to others. The real distinction here is earnings are generated without your active continual involvement—you are making money even when you are on vacation with this revenue stream!

The fourth and final, and I would suggest maybe the most important, revenue stream is that created from investment. A strong business must have a plan for how to invest the profits it makes either back into the business to grow that revenue stream or into vehicles outside the business which will provide financial security when you decide to stop working, unless you want to work forever!

The most successful business will develop strategies, products and services to capitalize on all four of these revenue models, or pillars as I sometimes call them. These four pillars are the foundation to business *and* financial success. Don't depend on just one of these streams of income—have all four working for you and achieve the success your efforts deserve!

Does Your Business Have Curb Appeal?

Corey Moore

Question: Would you eat a delicious steak off of a dirty plate?

In real estate, there is a term called 'curb appeal'. This means that many buyers make a decision on whether or not they will buy a particular home based on how the house looks on the outside, sometimes even before they see the inside. A house could not be sold if the outside doesn't look as beautiful as it does on the inside.

This happens all the time in business. You could have created a product that is the best thing since sliced bread, but if the representation of your business is not appealing, what is the likelihood of a potential client actually doing business with you and not your competitor?

Once we have created a great product, we forget that the only person on earth who knows its true value is us. We know that it is the best thing ever created; we know that it will truly help our clients; we know that our clients truly need it, but they don't know. How would they? They don't even know who we are, let alone what we produced. By definition, we are strangers to people who don't know us. Strangers don't typically approach other strangers unless they have a good reason to do so. We have to give them a sound reason, and surprisingly, it can't just be the product.

The average person is a 'visual' person. They enjoy looking at things that are aesthetically pleasing. They are more willing to approach something that is foreign to them if they like the way it looks. Business owners can use this information to their advantage by making the first thing that people see more appealing. That would be the business card and website.

Business Card: Other than you, typically the first thing a person sees about your business is your business card. Please know, they may not say it, but everyone judges your business based on your business card. If it doesn't look professional, they may feel you lack professionalism. If the info on it is incorrect, they may feel you are not detail-oriented. If it is on a very thin card stock, they may feel your product is cheap. If there is no design or it is very plain, they may think you lack creativity. All of these perceptions have nothing to do with your actual product, but it could be the difference of whether they buy it or not.

Website: Your website is like the virtual representation of your business. This is where a client needs to go and get a feel of exactly what you have to offer. The more they understand your product, the greater the chance that they'll become a client. In addition, the more time they spend visiting the site, as well as the degree to which they enjoy their experience, directly impacts whether or not they will become a client.

I am by no means suggesting that it is necessary to spend thousands of dollars on websites and business cards. Now, if you have the budget for it, by all means, do it. However, it is important to be very aware of the look and feel of your cards and site, as your goal is to attract potential clients. Your marketing materials should be visually appealing to create greater interest in your product. Your product/service is what will actually close the deal.

Biggest Mistakes Business Owners Make Because of Fear

Taneka Badie

Starting a business can be challenging when you don't know anything about starting a business. In my experience I free-lanced for three years before incorporating my business. I didn't know anything about planning or bookkeeping. I learned these things along the way. I would let myself into situations not knowing what I was really doing.

Make sure you have a business plan developed because this will help along your journey. A business plan is like a compass that helps you plan which directions to go with your business. Sometimes you may be going in the wrong direction, but if you get lost just take the necessary steps to reach your destination. **LivePlan** is a great tool to use for creating your business plan and tracking your progress. It breaks down the difficult process into simple steps. It also includes examples of each category so you understand how to write your business plan.

Keeping up with income and expenses is very important in business. For years I had a hard time with this, I think I just made it more difficult than it really was. I was so unorganized when it came to bookkeeping. **Intuit QuickBooks** is a great app that keeps track of your income, expenses, invoices, bills and much more.

Contracts can be scary to some people, but they are used to protect both parties. I got my first contract from a textbook so I wasn't sure if it included everything I needed to protect me in bad situations. Sometimes I didn't use contracts in the past because the clients felt like it was not necessary. That is something you should never agree to do. It is best to hire an attorney to look over your contracts. A lot of times we put off doing this because we think of the high costs. There are now subscription based legal services that are very affordable. So there is no excuse for you not to protect your business. The best time to do this is in the beginning stage of your business.

At the beginning of my career I was unsure of what to charge clients. I had little experience so I set my rates very low. As I got more experience I decided to increase my rates. I had many clients that wanted discounts because they had been working with me for years or referred others to my business. I gave them discounts because of my fear of losing clients or turning them away. It is best to talk to industry professionals about rates and do research. Later on, I realized cheaper is not always better. I had to work harder for $20 an hour vs. $75 an hour. Charge what you are worth based on your experience and other skills.

These are some common things that you should avoid. Always take the proper steps to protect your business. Having a plan is better than no plan at all because you will set goals that you are trying to reach. Never undervalue yourself. In order to succeed you must know your worth.

Stepping Over the Dollar to Pick Up the Dime

Dannella Burnett

As a business owner we are ALWAYS looking for ways to save money. The old saying is true, a penny saved is a penny earned. But too often we can get into the trap of trying to do it all because we CAN and not doing the things we SHOULD in order to keep costs in line!

For the first two years of my business I did my own bookkeeping. I knew that I needed an accountant to file my monthly sales taxes, payroll taxes and prepare monthly reports, but I decided that I would not use the bookkeeping services. I would save that money and do those tasks myself. Every month I would fill my dining room table with receipts, invoices, notes, proposals, quotes, check stubs....and spend 2 nights reading, reviewing, sorting, pondering, posting in a ledger, making notes of questions to ask my accountant or highlighting line items. It would take me 10-12 hours to finish the paperwork and enter everything into a computer ledger to turn over to my accountant each month.

When I'd been open about 2 years my accountant recommended I make the investment in QuickBooks and suggested hiring a QB Expert to set up my account. The QB Expert was also a bookkeeper. As we were going through the process of setting up my account we were reviewing my monthly activities and accounting needs and she let me know that based on my volume and activities she could do my monthly bookkeeping for $75. What! $75 vs 10-12 hours of work! I quickly signed on for her services and now use that time for other tasks that generate income or give me time freedom!! I know that I can easily earn well over $75 in a 10-12 hour period and monthly bookkeeping is not the best use of my time. Take a look at your activities, what generates income? What activities require your time and what can be outsourced or delegated to earn you dollars instead of saving dimes?

Some of the other activities you may consider looking at outsourcing are administrative tasks, social media marketing, running errands like shipping and shopping, research and organization. You might also consider some of your personal tasks like cleaning, lawn care, shopping, bill paying and find local companies or a concierge service that will help you better manage your time and resources.

So start paying the dime to earn the dollar!!

Know When to Clock Out

Tracee Randall

We have all seen it—the meme that shows the exhausted, overworked, stressed-to-the-max superwoman with briefcase in hand, children in tow, bathrobe flying, hair all askew—and the caption reads: "If you don't want the 9-5 be prepared to hustle 24/7!"

We all laugh to ourselves because deep down, we KNOW it's the truth! To be our own boss we gotta hustle, we gotta be willing to take risks—in the beginning we have to be the janitor, the director of marketing, the social media guru, the email writer, the one getting up early and staying up late. If you don't believe me, ask any one of these experts and they will tell you—it's true!

Is it worth it? I say, "yes" absolutely—but ONLY if you keep your priorities in place. This is sometimes easier said than done, and often it just slips up on you without you realizing it. There is another great tip in this book by JoBeth Martin, talking about some of these same points, titled "Gain the World Without Losing Your Soul"—and when I read it I thought, "YES"- this is a tip that is top of the list, and one that I have worked very hard on in the past to make sure I kept "in balance".

When my children were young (Ryan was about 6 years old, Robby was a 15 year old teenager), we owned an extremely profitable business in the relocation industry. We had over 100 corporate apartments and managed all the utilities, furniture rental, housewares, cable, and phone service for them—a full-time enterprise with 10 employees. We were generating over a 1/2 million dollars in sales each month, and had all the drama that comes along with a staff and corporate clients. We could have easily fallen into the trap of working 24/7, but the REASON I am an entrepreneur is to be able to SPEND TIME with my kids and my husband, right?? Even when our office was in our home (which it was for the first 5 years), I had an office dedicated to my business and (get this)—at 4pm when Ryan got off the school bus I was sitting on the front steps waiting on him! I walked away. My employees knew not to interrupt my "Mommy-Time" and I had leveraged my time by putting together a great team!

I planned it that way—I worked hard when I worked, but I knew how to punch the clock when my *priorities* arrived home. Most small business owners don't do this. In fact, my husband would forget the "rules" and we would be sitting on the sofa when the kids were both in bed and he would bring up the subject of "work". Unless it was a true emergency (which it seldom was) I would gently remind him that I was "off the clock" and we could talk about it in the morning! I set boundaries and this was a great thing.

Many small business owners are under the impression that when they are their own boss they will have more time freedom—but typically that is not the case. We do have the flexibility to make our own hours, to work around the lives of our families, but the struggle is real. It's a balancing act. It's easy to get so caught up in making a living that we forget to live.

No matter what is going on in your business, you will be stronger and healthier if you set those priorities—whatever they are—and stick to them. Every one of us could easily work at our business 24/7, but I challenge you to set those parameters and do your best to stick with them. YOU will be healthier, more creative, more satisfied and your business will prosper!

I will admit, as the kids grew older and became adults, I did extend my hours and I have absolutely allowed priorities to slip at times, but when I do I always go back to this #1 "rule"—God first, family second, business third. That formula has never failed me. Know when to "clock out."

Don't Compare Your Beginning to Someone Else's Middle

Deborah Daniel

We compare ourselves to others—it's a fact we cannot avoid. We look around us and think—that person is skinnier, wealthier, funnier—whatever we want more of. You do it in business as well, even if you won't admit it! This can be dangerous when you are first getting started or it can help you take it to the next level even faster. Often when I speak to groups of entrepreneurs people want to know how I have navigated being in business for 23 years and how I have gained such a large client base and community. My answer is always the same—a lot of time and a lot of work! Not too long ago I watched an interview with billionaire entrepreneur Mark Cuban done by Sandra Yancey, founder and CEO of eWomenNetwork, where she asked Mark why he thought most entrepreneurs do not make it in business. I totally agree with his reply- "Most people are not willing to do the work". Entrepreneurship is not a free ticket to wealth or an invitation to sit back and watch the cash register ring.

In the beginning you have to be willing to do just about anything that needs to be done in your business—I know I was. When I opened my first tax office my husband and I painted the walls of a little rental space, rented some office furniture and even hung our own sign on the outside. Fortunately we picked a great location because we signed the lease with no customers, no advertising in place and only the knowledge of how to do what we were selling! Knowing what I know now I would never have jumped in with so little preparation, but 23 years later I can see that the hard work paid off!

The important thing is don't compare yourself to someone with a mature business and think you don't measure up in the very early days of your business. You weren't there when that person was sitting in an office with newly rented furniture waiting for the first person to stop in! Do the work—that's what really counts—the success will follow in direct proportion to the effort!

Leave It to the Pros

Stephanie Combes

DIY (Do It Yourself) is for HGTV, NOT for running your business. In order to run a successful business, you have to be aware of the pieces of the puzzle that you may not have mastered on your own. This is entirely okay! Struggle is pivotal to success. You must recognize when it is time to pass things on and let it go! Don't be afraid to find someone who can do it better. This could range anywhere from hiring a designer for your logo, a bookkeeper or a financial advisor for your next best step economically, or entrusting someone to put the well-constructed chaos of your thoughts into words that can more easily be deciphered, like I have done here:

"My name is Bre, or as Stephanie calls me 'Breezy'. I am the voice behind Stephanie Combes. Stephanie was a Marketing Manager at the restaurant I work for. She immediately began brainstorming ideas on how to get our brand in other people's and other businesses' mouths. She took a business that was struggling to be known and paired it with ideas that would get our customers excited about something as simple as a burger. One of her ideas was taking our two sous chefs and throwing them into a battle of culinary creativity to create the bestselling burger.

"I saw her laptop sitting on a table one day and was immediately enticed by the blinking cursor that was staring back at me. I ranted on for a few sentences about the competition, the stakes, (or steaks rather), in an effortless buoyant tone. In my mind, I was just playing around with some words. When Stephanie read it, it transformed into something else in her own head. What was easy for me, was an opportunity for her. She fell in love with the way I placed words into sentences. She believed that I had a gift and was eager to collaborate. We went on to join forces in building the mobile bank phenomenon that is *Instatricity*. I took the otherwise blasé aspects of introducing a new project and played with the readers' minds instead, through the use of quirky blogs and fun fact emails. It made a facile and necessary piece of equipment a toy that could be enjoyed as well as being practical. This is fun for me and a passion of mine. I was thrilled when she asked me to be her creative voice in this book and trusted me to write about her business endeavors that she is insatiably proud of. All it takes is one person to recognize what you're capable of and I am honored to continue this journey with a wonderful friend of mine. My final note on this business tip, Pros don't have to be in the yellow pages. Sometimes the pros are the people in our lives that just need a mirror in front of their very own special gifts."

~ Bre Belardinelli

Barter is Better and Better Bartering

Dannella Burnett

Barter has been used as a currency for exchange for eons... rural doctors exchange services for their patient's chickens and other farm produce, the promoter exchanges tickets for advertising, early western furriers traded furs for food and staples... today businesses exchange their products and services with other businesses and everyone gets what they want and need, right? Let's take a look.

When two people or two businesses exchange with each other it's called direct barter and it does work. It works well if two people or two businesses have similar value products or services and have a need for the other one in a similar time frame. But what if the doctor has too many chickens or the farmer has excess livestock and produce but doesn't need the doc this week? This is one of the challenges with direct barter, you may not find the value in the other person's exchange and they may not want your products or services when you have them available. One side of the transaction may end up with items they don't need and may feel the exchange was less valuable or may not be able to find the product or service needed when you have excess inventory or time to offer. Or the worst case scenario, the other person/business doesn't come through with their end of the bargain... we've probably all had that happen too many times.

So what is the answer? How do you move excess inventory, share your products and services with new clients that want what you have when you have it and know that you're getting all your value? Join an organized Barter Network. It removes the direct barter element and allows you to trade when and with what you want to and allows you to spend when you have a need. Typically barter "dollars" are tracked through accounting software and there is a small fee for the network to oversee and manage the accounts.

For example...I sell $1000 of wedding services to a bride that owns a furniture store. They earned their trade dollars selling 10 bar stools to a new restaurant in town. The restaurant earned their trade dollars offering 20 $50 gift certificates to the network. Twenty different businesses bought those certificates with trade dollars they earned in 20 different industries. The cycle is endless as the networks grow and everyone uses the offers that are a fit for them. As for Barter Networks there are several all across the nation and even several within major metropolitan areas and all may have slightly different guidelines and businesses they represent, so as always you'll want to do your due diligence. I've been involved with a barter network here in Atlanta for the past 5 years and have had a great experience with nearly $200K in business I've traded in that time.

I've traded my catering services, wedding and event planning, our gourmet healthy coffee, our decadent fudge, my husband's plumbing services, some excess linens and other catering equipment, rented Chocolate Fountains, business consulting services, wedding cakes, vendor and sponsor opportunities and more, whatever is ours to offer and the time is right to offer on barter. In exchange we have used our barter dollars to pay for our kids' afterschool program, dental work, vacations, jewelry, sponsorships, advertising, holiday gifts, massages, printing, signage, hair styling, circus and show tickets and so much more. In addition every time I perform a service for a barter client, I'm also getting exposure to new clients including cash clients – it's a Win-Win-Win!

Barter is better than allowing excess inventory to sit on the shelf or become an unsalable commodity, or allowing time spent idle that could generate income on barter. Barter is also a great way to grow your business. I definitely recommend participating with a quality-based, reputable barter network where your products and services are promoted and exchanged at the correct value and monies are exchanged using software that is easily tracked and transacted.

Make Failure Your Best Friend

Deborah Daniel

I read an article recently that proposed that fear was the biggest obstacle in reaching success in business. Not lack of skill, not lack of contacts, not lack of a sound business model or marketing strategy—but rather FEAR is stifling the success of many businesses. This article was referring to women in business but based on consulting with both men and women for nearly 25 years—I can emphatically say that women do not have a monopoly on fear in business or life!

With my clients and in fact my own business I call this Analysis Paralysis. Often when we were deciding to purchase a product or service for the business or even hire a new team member, a LOT of time was spent researching, looking at options and ultimately in fear of making the wrong decision we put off making a decision so long that when we were ready to act the circumstances had already changed and the whole cycle of researching and evaluating started again. This only results in a whole lot of time spent not doing things that make money for your business. Once I decided to break this cycle I definitely saw my business take off and I have seen my clients do the same thing.

The culture I adopted—and I encourage new businesses to jump on quickly—is to act more swiftly and more often. Imperfect action towards your objectives and goals always trumps a perfect plan that is never implemented. Alternately adopt the habit of acting, reviewing the results and making course correction as needed. I certainly would never advocate hasty decisions with no prior thought but I do encourage you to plan, do and review, so that making decisions becomes as second nature as chewing your food before swallowing. Each action moves you to the next fork in the road and another set of potential decisions and outcomes. When you adopt this habit of acting more quickly you will stop considering any outcome a failure but rather consider it just more information to make the next decision better and faster. I would encourage you to Fail Forward until you reach your goals!

Change Your WORDS – Change Your WORLD

Mark A. Sterling

"If there is no enemy within, the enemy outside can do you no harm!"

African Proverb

Words are more than just the essentials of speech or writing. They can be used to affect how energy is transmitted. When spoken out loud, words *transform* into vibrations. Change your vibe – Change your tribe. Change your WORDS – Change your WORLD.

There is so much power in words. We see this in the 3 words 'I love you' that everyone wants to hear, and in the 3 words that can blemish even the strongest person; "I hate you".

Did you know that scientists have found that just hearing sentences (words) about elderly people led research subjects to walk more slowly? Also, individuals that read words of 'loving kindness' showed increases in self-compassion, improved mood, and reduced anxiety.

I once read that a word is like a living organism, capable of growing, changing, spreading, and influencing the world in many ways, directly and indirectly through others. I never thought about a word being 'alive' but it makes sense.

Proverbs 18:21 states "Death and life are in the power of the tongue, and those who love it will eat its fruits". Of course, the "tongue" in this verse represents that which tongues produce: Words.

Words are the seeds for new beginnings. Plant good seeds on fertile ground. Words allow us to affirm our future before it arrives. Words can paint bold beautiful pictures on the canvas of our imaginations.

Speak what you see until you see what you said.

Always Be Networking

Corey Moore

Thought: If People = Resources = Solutions = Growth = Success, then People must equal Success.

The one thing that I have learned during my years in business is that 100% of all businesses that went out of business ran into a problem they could not solve. Everyone knows that, as a business owner, you are going to encounter problems. Therefore, you now have to make sure that you arm yourself with as many solutions as possible.

People: Every business needs multiple types of people....whether these people work in the business, are clients of the business, are service providers to the business, are consultants for the business, are referral sources to the business, etc. Since every person represents a different role for the business, you must find enough people to fill all of these roles.

Resources: Every person has a certain value attached to them, which makes them resources. That value is determined by the role they play in the business when a problem arises. When a large order needs to be filled, more hands are needed. When there is a revenue problem, clients are needed. When there is a company awareness problem, marketing is needed. When a fork in the road is present, a consultant is needed to brainstorm decisions. When trying to get accepted in a specific circle or group, a referral partner is needed.

Solutions: Take any of the problems above and imagine having a person there that can solve the problem. You could lose a client if you don't deliver a finished product on time. Every paying client is now cash flow for a business. Having money for marketing is important because if a potential buyer can't find you, they can't give you money. There are problems that arise in business that money can't solve. For these problems, it takes mind power. The more minds working on a problem, the more possible solutions are found; when you have fewer minds, you have fewer solutions. Sometimes knowing the right people can get you into a door that you would not be able to open by yourself. If you don't know the right person, you are stuck outside!

Growth: Every time a business comes across a problem, the business metaphorically stops. It cannot continue until it finds a solution. Find more help, continue. Find a client, continue. Get more marketing out, continue. Brainstorm and find the solution, continue. Get introduced to the decision maker, continue. Not being able to succeed in any of these could result in you eventually closing your doors.

Success: The more solutions, the more growth. Success can be achieved if you continue to grow. This is the land of milk and honey that every entrepreneur is trying to reach. Most entrepreneurs never reach this place.

The Ultimate Solution = Meet More People: You never know how a person will affect your business, we just know that we need as many people as possible. Make sure that everywhere you go, you let people know what your business does and what its needs are. The beauty is, they will tell you exactly how they can help you.

Interns are More Than Just Cheap Labor

Dannella Burnett

Interns can be a great way to lower labor costs for projects and your business, but it's important to know the other costs associated with bringing in interns and creating an environment that benefits the intern as well. As an event and hospitality company we have had many approach us to be either a paid or unpaid intern to learn the ins and outs of our company and this has been a mutually beneficial relationship. We have also been an intern site for the last 4 years for Project Success, a local organization that works with Special Needs Young Adults to provide them work-force experience and life skills.

While we have enjoyed the benefit of paying zero or below market wages for staff, we have compensated with time, education and experience for the interns that allows them to move on to the next level of schooling or employment or sometimes, just as valuable, discovery for the interns that this type of work is not what they envisioned!

One of the most successful uses of interns was a project that we had when we really expanded the business in terms of the number of employees and moved into a new venue with a coffee shoppe and a café. We knew that we needed a very comprehensive employee manual with job descriptions, policies, practices and lots of legal information to be in compliance with state agencies and employment practices. We approached the local university and hired 2 interns in Human Resource Management /Business Studies and put them to the task, overseen by their professor to help us write an employment manual that would be comprehensive and legal within our state. Once done, we had our attorney review it, but it was a great project for the students and a HUGE cost savings for our company.

The kids that come on our site during the school year with Project Success have been a joy and a blessing as well. As we have taught them valuable work skills that they can use in jobs in the hospitality industry, we've had the pleasure of seeing a group of young adults that would fall through the cracks without an opportunity such as this. This is a benefit to our community as well as to our company.

The important thing to remember with interns is there must be a benefit to them to work for reduced or no pay, a benefit of education, training or certification, and the specific roles must be defined. If implemented well, interns can be a valuable resource for a business as it grows or has projects that need extra hands or extra attention.

Balloons and Bears

Tracee Randall

I started my first "real" business when I was 24-years-old, newly married and 6 months pregnant! My desire was to stay home with my new baby, but in truth I believe I was born with an entrepreneurial spirit. In 1984 there was not a consignment store on every corner as there is today. I had always shopped garage sales, and every Friday and Saturday I would map out my route from the ads in the newspaper and follow the signs that sprang up on the street corners every Thursday afternoon. I came home with treasures to fill the baby's room—"barely used" items that cost me pennies on the dollar!

As my husband and I sat around the kitchen table discussing my job options, it came to me that maybe I could create an income by reselling the garage sale items for more than I bought them for—and within weeks I had found a location, collected enough inventory to get started and opened my doors for business. Now your thoughts might be—"so what?" Today with consignment stores by the dozen, Ebay, Craig's List and all the internet opportunities to sell and resell maybe you're not too impressed. Read on!

When it came to naming our new business we struggled. After tossing around some potential names and with our doors opening within days, we finally settled on "Balloons and Bears"—a decision that turned out to be extremely profitable in an unexpected way. Several months after our Grand Opening it was time for our local phone books to be delivered (yes, I am dating myself). Sales were great, location was good, lots of inventory and I was able to keep my newborn at the shop with me and we were making a profit.

With the arrival of the thick "white pages" on every doorstep, one rather quiet afternoon in the shop I answered the phone, "Balloons and Bears!" A woman's voice, "Yes, I wanted to check your prices for a balloon delivery this Saturday for my daughter's 4th birthday party?"

What happened next changed everything. I looked over at the helium tank and the brightly colored balloons I had blown up that morning scattered around the shop. "Sure!" I answered. "I can deliver a balloon bouquet." My mind was quickly calculating the cost of 8 balloons, the helium and the like-new stuffed animal we could use to hold it down.

"We charge $20." I heard myself say—then held my breath waiting for an answer.

"Perfect!" I heard the woman reply and I exhaled. "Oh—do you have a clown that can deliver too?"

"Of course! But the clown is $20 extra." Well, I was our first clown, but the rest is history! We went on to grow into the largest, most profitable character balloon delivery service in our city—and each character, each idea was based on a NEED the client brought to us. I did my best to never say the words "No, we don't have that" to a client. If the client asked if we had a dancing bear for example (we WERE Balloons and BEARS after all), I made the decision then and there that we would satisfy that client's need. I did most of the deliveries myself in the beginning (hint hint—a small business owner wears multiple hats—or costumes—in the beginning stages) but as we grew our staff grew! In a few months we had 10 part-time employees and 5 full-time employees, and because we were known in the city for creating new and innovative balloon and character deliveries, our business spread through word of mouth! The whole city was talking about our characters. We quickly transitioned out of the used baby clothes business to a whole new arena which was more profitable and more exciting as well.

The point of this tip is that as small business owners we must be flexible—sometimes our ideas are great, but when we LISTEN to the needs of our prospects or potential clients the possibilities are endless! Too many small business owners cling to their business plan and aren't willing to be flexible enough to change. Ask yourself, what need can I fill and how can I do it differently? Then get going!

What Just Happened Here??

JoBeth Martin

Whether we like it or not we are bringing our whole self with all of our life experiences to our business. Usually that is a very good thing. We each have our own unique life experiences and have grown in amazing ways to get to where we are as successful individuals. But what about the things that aren't so pretty, the things that we would rather forget? I am afraid that they are still there too and often show up at the most inopportune times.

You may be thinking, how in the world does this apply to building a business and making a profit? Most of the time it won't. You may be able to push through the hard stuff, overcome the failures and act like you have it all together. That will work almost all of the time for most people. But I want to challenge that sometimes you get surprised by an emotion, a reaction that you have to a situation that totally comes out of the blue. It feels like you have been whacked upside the head by a two-by-four and you don't know what hit you. All of a sudden the pushing through and overcoming the hard stuff just doesn't work when you feel paralyzed by this weird emotion or reaction. What do you do with that?

Here is a truth for you; if something causes a very strong emotion in you that seems inconsistent with the situation you are in, take a little time to think through why you are reacting that way. Usually you will find that the emotion is really tied to something difficult, hurtful or fearful in the past that caused deep emotion. The present situation is simply a trigger that causes the emotion to resurface. If you can step back and work through this process it will give you the opportunity to act out of choice instead of "reacting" from emotion. You may find that you are saved from reacting in a way that may hurt your reputation, a relationship and even your business.

Otherwise, you either just suck it up and "act" like everything is "ok" or you may react to the perceived issue that really is not an issue at all. By doing this you are not being your best and authentic self and bringing your "A" game to the business situation. I experienced this personally just a few months ago and how I reacted hopefully impacted my business in a positive way instead of negative.

I was at a networking event and something was said to me that immediately caused a lot of hurtful emotion. I was totally confused because the statement was really neutral and was not in itself hurtful at all. I was surprised by the intensity of the emotion I felt and I immediately shut down. After a short time it began to make sense. The statement hit on a hurt that was actually based on a lie that had been spoken repeatedly in my heart for several years prior. My emotion was based on past events that caused great pain, not on the present situation.

Why is something like this even important in business? Because we are human and sometimes have broken places. If I had not recognized the broken place from the past and stopped to pray about and consider the truth I would very likely have reacted to that person. A person who did not deserve my reaction and a person who I dearly respect and love. In fact, a person who has been of incredible value to my life and business. I am grateful that I stopped and asked, "WHAT JUST HAPPENED HERE?"

Success is Scheduled

Deborah Daniel

Success in business rarely happens by chance. Talent or expertise, charisma and even being at the right place at the right time can bring some level of success, but usually these attributes can only take you so far. I am sure you have encountered friends or colleagues that seem like they have everything going for them to be a superstar in their field but never quite achieve it.

The one thing I think keeps entrepreneurs from that pinnacle we are all striving for is probably something most people overlook. While most of us are good at being guardians of our wealth—or at least I hope you are—most people waste too much of perhaps our most precious resource—time!

In working with small businesses the most common objection I hear for not implementing strategies to improve their business is not that they do not have the money to do it but they don't have the time. I think this speaks directly to the problem that as a business owner you must work on your business and not in it. If you were to write down everything you did in a day for a week and then highlight the items that only you could do in the business, I bet hardly anything would be highlighted. Most of us wander through the day with no plan letting endless interruptions from phone, email or texts   and the unwillingness to delegate tasks sidetrack us even if we had a plan—which most of us don't.

I love a To Do list and frankly I am guilty of adding an item if I do something that wasn't on the list just because I like to mark it off! The problem with this is we get caught up in the busy-ness of our business instead of focusing on the truly important tasks. You have to find a way to make sure you are focusing on your highest priority activities. The strategies I use to stop this endless cycle: Time block and know the must do actions for the next day before I leave the office.

Time blocking has been a life saver in my business. In an effort to be responsive to my clients I took every call and looked at every email as soon as it came in regardless of what I was working on at the time—this resulted in having to review and start over on the same things multiple times before I finished a project. Instead, pick two or three breaks in the day when you will return calls and answer emails. This will allow you to complete more in less time because you do not have to spend as much time figuring out where you left off!

The really important tasks don't happen if you wait to find time. You won't follow up on that proposal, make the sales call, or go to that networking event if you don't schedule the time to do these things. If you wait until you get started for the day to list out what is a MUST for that day it does not ever happen—you get to the office, start looking at emails, problems come up, phone calls come in and the next thing you know the day is over and you never made the list for the day! The last task of the day should be writing your plan for the next day. Your feet hit the floor in the morning and you know the meeting you have and the projects that need to be completed. Don't waste your most precious resource—time. Mastery of your time will give you the slight edge that leads to super success!

Don't Like Selling? Try Telling!

Corey Moore

Here is a story of how most people start a business:

Let's say I make a really good cookie. I have been baking ever since my mother taught me how. Over the years I have studied different types of baking techniques, experimented with several recipes, and sought out to taste every type of cookie that has ever been conceived.

Currently, I know how to make many types of cookies, I have eight that will knock your socks off.

Every time someone tries one of my cookies, they would say the same thing 'Wow, this is a great cookie. You should start a business and sell these.'

Start a business? I have always made cookies because it was just something I loved to do. Start a business? It was a stress reliever, therapeutic, and most of all, fun. Start a business? It always reminds me of the times that I spent watching my mom cook or when she was teaching me her cooking secrets. A business...never really thought about it like that.

Hmmm, start a business...why not?! It's a passion of mine and I don't feel the same way when I am in the office as I do when I am in the kitchen. Why not! Everyone likes my cookies when they try them. They all say they would buy them if I were to sell them. Why not?! I know everything there is to know about cookies. I am going to start a business!!

Does this sound familiar? This is typically how someone starts their business. They then quickly find out that making cookies and the 'Cookie Making Business' are two completely different things. Doing something as a hobby which has no expectations is very different than having to sell a certain amount of product, to make a certain amount of money, to pay specific bills. It doesn't take long to discover the need for more clients. The warm circle of family and friends has run out and now it is time to sell to the general public. But wait, no one said anything about having to sell to anyone. I am not a sales person, I just make cookies.

If you are in this boat, I have a great technique that will keep people buying your product and you won't have to give any sales presentations. Stop selling your cookies and start telling people what you know about cookies. Tell people what the difference is between one cookie versus another. Tell people which cookies are good for individuals with certain allergies. Tell people which cookie compliments certain foods or drinks. Tell people which cookies are healthier than others.

People will begin to view you as an expert in the cookie field. Once they find out that you actually make cookies, they will assume that the taste is probably just as amazing as your knowledge. They will typically ask to purchase before you can even tell them they are for sale.

Does this technique actually work? I am proud to say that I built my accounting firm to 250 clients in 3 years just by telling people that I did taxes and could answer any question that they had. I take great pride in knowing that I did not have to sell one person on using my services.

In business, sales are required, selling isn't. Do what is more comfortable to you. It will continue to be your passion and not another job.

Find Worth Other Than Monetary Value

Stephanie Combes

No one gets rich overnight. Well, some people do, but some people think unicorns exist too. Money can't be your only reason for starting a business. You have to see the light in other parts. It is important to stay humble. You are starting from the ground up. It's easy to get lost in a sea of dollar signs.

I talk about investments in different increments. You may not always grab the sale right away, you may not always walk away from an event with a client. I would bet good money though, that you walked away with other value, whether it be a life lesson, mentorship, PR, press, valuable information, referrals, or creative ideas, just to name a few. I have donated my time, money and efforts to many non-profits and community outreach programs, I have taken low paying jobs to learn new trades, I have traveled far to meet and support people.

One of my most valuable relationships here in Atlanta is with that of a co-author in this book, Dannella Burnett, an award winning event planner. I had barely heard Dannella's name when I knew she was someone I wanted to reach. I picked up the phone one day to see how we could work together and she accepted an invitation for me to visit, and we never looked back. I had to invest an hour drive each way to work with her, but the mentorship, friendship, and business collaborations were far worth that investment every single time.

The rewards from each of my business deals have showered me in more ways than I could have hoped for. I gained respect, awareness, friendships, collaborations and more. If your heart is removed, you will never succeed. Your heart is what builds the connections that keep your business afloat. More zeroes in a bank account is ideal, but you'll stop seeing good in anything else if that's all this is for. Yes, it's a business. However, sacrificing a few dollars to remember your roots is important too.

Love what you do and always remember why your started. If you do that, you will still gain those zeroes in your account, and you will do it with less weight on your shoulders. You will prosper as you remember there are other happiness factors in building your company as well.

Event Marketing - Does It Make Sense and Make Dollars?

Dannella Burnett

We have many ways to advertise and market our business and it's important to know the costs and value of each type of marketing. There are many that include print, radio, social, relational, email, internet and event marketing. One area we have focused on is event marketing. The cost per exposure can be very low and the benefit of being front and center to a potential client and having a live conversation can create an excellent selling and exposure opportunity.

Here are some questions that you need to ask when looking at events to determine if you should participate:

1. What is the reason for the event?
2. Is this the first time this event has been produced?
3. What is the cost and what does that cost include (space, table, chairs, table cloths, signage, advertising, hospitality, opportunity to speak to audience, opportunity to get database of attendees, opportunity for sponsorships or increased visibility, exposure before or after the event on social media or email campaigns....)
4. What is the time commitment for the event?
5. How many attendees are expected?
6. What is the demographic of the attendees expected?
7. How is the event being advertised?
8. Is the event indoors or outdoors? If outdoors, what are any weather plans?
9. Can you include your items in a goody bag or raffle for increased exposure?
10. Where is event located and how best to load/unload your products?
11. How many other vendors will be there and who are they?

A good planner will answer many of these questions in the initial offer for vendor spaces or in the vendor package so always read all the information available to you before sending this list of questions or picking up the phone. An informed vendor is usually a happy vendor so be sure to get this information so you are participating in the events that make sense for you. Remember it must make sense to make dollars!

Once you decide to participate in an event, the way you participate is also critical. We teach an entire course on maximizing your vendor opportunities but some key points are...

1. A visually appealing display.
2. Clear information for the attendees passing your display.
3. An engaging offer, activity or sample at your table to get the passerby to stop.
4. A way of "ethically bribing" the attendees to give you their information for follow up.
5. The ability to sell your product, service or special either onsite or online.
6. A pleasant and engaging personality with everyone that comes to your table.
7. A reason for the attendee to do business with you or want to follow up.
8. A plan for following up with an email campaign, card or phone call.

The fortune is truly in the follow-up, so number 8 is critical. We have 3 follow up practices that we use following vendor events that when put into practice make the money and time invested in vendor opportunities make sense AND make dollars.

The Number One Vital Sign for a Healthy Business

Tracee Randall

For the past 10 years I have ALWAYS put my health first. It's so easy, especially as women entrepreneurs, to forego our own needs and health because we are nurturers—we naturally take care of others. I am going to shock you by making this statement, *"the woman who puts her business or others first before her own health is actually the **most selfish**."* Why? Because what happens when the Mom breaks down? What happens to the family and the business when the Mom is lying in bed sick with a migraine? What happens when Mom isn't there because she is too sick to move or too stressed?? EVERYTHING falls apart.

In 2007 I was in that place—hormonal imbalance, depression, panic and anxiety attacks, carpal tunnel pain in both my hands and arms, strep throat at least once a year—and I would be considered "healthy"! I never missed a day's work, never stopped, always at the top of my game! However, I was introduced to an incredible nutritional supplement that literally changed my health AND the health of my family forever. Like most women in business, I never allowed these issues to stop me, and probably never would have sought out nutrition for myself—but my oldest son Robby had been born with skin issues that controlled our lives—he itched 24 hours per day, 7 days per week, so along with my businesses, church volunteering, and everything else, I was on a mission to help him heal. We had started out in the medical field, leaving no stone unturned, but his immune system crashed and he was left hopeless by the doctors. As all mothers do when their child is suffering, I was not willing to stop until we found a solution for Robby's disease.

The answer came through a product in the direct sales industry (which by the way, makes the best nutritional products in the world) – and within 2 weeks of Robby using this product he was 75% symptom-free of a 22 year disease AND he told me, "Mom, I was lying in bed last night and I just started to cry; it's the first time I've ever felt comfortable in my own skin." 6 months later Robby was 95% symptom free—which was amazing—but at the same time, **SO WAS I**! I felt like a million bucks—and I knew that I would never go back to feeling the way I had been! Since that time, I became aligned with the nutritional protocols of the American Anti-Cancer Institute as well as the International Wellness & Research Center and have been blessed to have helped hundreds of people with their health!

As a small business owner or entrepreneur our #1 priority **has** to be our health. And unfortunately quite often we put our health or self-care on the back burner as we build our wealth and fortune. Sadly, I have seen too many incredible businesses crumble because the owner became ill—and we all know the statistics—disease and hospital bills are the number 1 reason for bankruptcy in the world today.

The health statistics in the United States are staggering. The truth of the matter is, it is very likely that we will experience a debilitating disease. Here are the facts—according to the American Cancer Society—1 in 2 men will be diagnosed with cancer, 1 in 3 women, AND it is now the #1 killer of our children today.

So that's the bad news—what's the *good news*? What's the tip? The tip is that it is up to us to take control of our own health. It's up to us to rise up out of mediocrity and fight for what is ours—**our health**! HOW? It truly is simple. Boost your immune system by using a DAILY SUPPLEMENT.

According to the AACI, if we can create a strong immune system, our bodies will ALWAYS be able to fight disease. I have a simple 10 step guide available at no cost on my website that helps locate an extra $150 in EVERYONE'S budget that can be spent on nutrition that will boost and build the immune system. As a wellness coach since 2007 I have helped hundreds of small business owners who realized that their HEALTH comes first, and that when their health fails, their business fails. I have watched way too many entrepreneurs fail to check for the vital signs of a healthy business—and the first and most important one is YOU. It's just that simple.

Change is Good

Mark A. Sterling

We have all heard that old adage that 'Change is good but growth is optional', but many of us have never been taught how to change.

Change Is The Bridge To A New Season In Your Life.

Seasons change. Jobs change. Friends change. Even we change. We MUST embrace and anticipate change.

Change happens by influence or by intent. We move through awareness, acceptance to action.

Awareness

Until there is a conscious recognition for the need to change, we will have no reason to make changes. As a matter of fact, many of us do not know that that there is a need to change in order to meet or become our better self

Think about it. How do we change what we don't even know exists? Changing what I don't even know exists is tough. It won't matter how many other people recognize the need, no meaningful change will be embarked upon until we consciously recognize the need.

Changing what I don't even know exists is tough.

NOTE: Not everything in life needs to be changed or should be changed. The continuous process of personal growth through self-development will assist us in knowing why, if and when things should be changed.

Acceptance

This is an important momentum and critical mass milestone; people shift from seeing the change as something "out there," to seeing it as having personal relevance. This perspective enables them to make decisions about accepting or not accepting their part in the change.

You will know you are here when you begin to think, *"However we got here is unimportant – it is what it is. Let's figure out how to navigate the future with the tools and advantages we've got, not what we wish we had."* With acceptance comes peace, a sense of calm, and the ability to think clearly and take actions.

It's been my experience that the people who are further along in the process tend to catch grief from the people who are not. I ask that you be as respectful as possible of those who are in a slightly different place with all this. Know that where they are is right where they need to be at this moment. We can all benefit tremendously from supporting each other through this process.

If you blame others for your losses, you must also blame others for your wins. You see, if we take credit for winning, we must also ACCEPT responsibility for losing. There is power in personal acceptance.

Five Rules for Accepting

1. Accept totally the role of student and follower - don't let your ego stand between you and your learning.
2. Ask the right questions.
    a. Don't forget the chain of solution.
    b. Find out what you can do to solve the issue.
    c. Purposefully ask questions that stimulate your own growth.
3. Immediately put into action what has been taught/learned.
4. Be disciplined in dealing with your coach/mentor.
    a. Use their time wisely.
    b. Set up appointments in advance.
5. Be committed to the process. Never threaten to give up.

Action

Action? No, I just wanted to use another 'A' word. I actually call the
third step – "RECONDITIONING" re·con·di·tion [ˌrēkən ˈdiSH(ə)n,
A verb meaning to condition again, overhaul or renovate; to make like]
When we recondition our minds, we prepare it for new thoughts, new
beliefs and new possibilities.

You are probably asking, how do we recondition our minds? The short
answer is a strong belief system (faith) coupled with repetitious
information.

In Napolean Hill's book *"Think and Grow Rich"* he states: *"Repetition of
affirmation of orders to your subconscious mind is the only known
method of voluntary development of the emotion of faith."*

Turn your car into "Drive Time University". Listen to only personally
empowering information while you are driving and as much as possible
while you are at home or work.

You can't mix water (new thoughts, beliefs and possibilities) with oil
(old limiting thoughts and negative associations. You must displace the
old with the new. You must saturate your subconscious mind
(*"Repetition of affirmation of orders)* with new empowering
information.

Allow Yourself Time To Change.

Everyone fails. The ONLY difference is that winners simply DECIDE to
get back up... and keep moving toward their own personal finish lines.
Don't be too hard on yourself. Step by step you will start noticing
the Rewards of Change.

*Discomfort will be your opposition for change. "The Lord upholdeth all
that fall, and raiseth up all that be bowed down" (Psalm 145:14)*

TIPS ON BRANDING

"Your brand is the single most
important investment
you can make in your business."

~ Steve Forbes

Consistency

Ires D. Alliston

Consistency is important in everything you do. It establishes familiarity and recognition.

Be consistent with your business name, logo, and the colors you use for each. Just like artists, musician and authors should use the same photo for every social media account, so should businesses use the same logo as their profile picture on every account. This also makes it easy for someone who "likes" your Facebook page to find you on Twitter, etc.

Be consistent in the layout of your website. If visitors to your site see the navigation menu and sidebars on your homepage and they look the same on every page of your site, it will not only look nice, it may also help lower your bounce rate. The only exception to consistency on websites is your landing page specifically set-up to collect leads or email addresses. Now having said that, whatever image and style you use on your landing page should also be consistent with everything else that agrees with your brand.

Be consistent with your blog. Although some brands who have multiple writers for their blog have some leeway with this, the overall message of your blog should continue or align with the theme of your brand's core values. The best blog writers gain such a massive following because they have an entertaining, engaging, and *consistent* personality that comes through in every post. If someone writes a very sarcastic blog post one week and it gets a ton of shares, then writes a blog with a very dry humor the following week, it may confuse readers and they may just be disappointed with that same person!

Be consistent with the tone of voice you use in emails. If you have a professional tone for your blog posts, keep it professional. If you also want to add a little humor to the mix, please do so; however, do not go overboard. Now, if you jump around and meander aimlessly, customers and readers will get bored, get confused and opt out.

Definitely be consistent in the tone of voice in your social media posts. Your audience will start to look forward to your next social media post when you deliver the type of valuable, funny, or informative social media post time and time again. It might get boring to you after you write a thousand of the same structured posts, but your fans and followers will see the consistency and will appreciate it more!

I would even go so far as to say be as consistent as possible in the font and size of text you use anytime you write something that is going to be read by your audience. However, this is not always necessary. Depending on what you're trying to do or accomplish, just make sure you stay close to your brand. For example, when I create posts for my social channels, I'm creative with my graphics and use alternative texts to create emphasis but remain consistent with my brand and theme.

Last but not least, be consistent in your overall *élan*. The way you bring everything together in a way that represents who you are, what you do, and why you're doing it should be immediately discernable by any of your customers. And once you have that down, you're well on your way to becoming the world's next highly-successful brand. Congratulations!

Your Twitter Brand: Key to Influence and Opportunities

Angela Hemans

You are what you tweet! Every tweet you publish is a 140 character representation of you and what you want to share with the world. If you don't want it to be attached to your brand, then think before you tweet it. Who would have thought that tweets can create such an impact? Take a moment to think about any celebrity or politician that was impacted negatively because of a tweet they sent.

How Do You Create A Twitter Brand Worth Tweeting About? You're the foundation of your brand whether you're creating one on Twitter or any social media platform. Consider this before you create a calendar of Twitter content, and before you begin scheduling your tweets. What do you want to be known for? What is your area of expertise that you want to share with your Twitter community? What are your unique skills that others can appreciate? Take a moment and put it all together, everything should align with you, your business, your marketing and sales strategy. Now that you have all the pieces of the puzzle, how does marketing on Twitter fit into that puzzle? What kind of content is consistent with your brand?

Building a Twitter Brand Is a Journey, When I first started using Twitter, I met many great people and had tons of interesting conversations and although I was growing my following, I had no real brand strategy and no one knew what I did and how I could help them. Once I realized my mistake, I had to figure out where I was and where I wanted to go using Twitter.

Here are 4 simple landmarks to help you brand yourself:

1. Is my mission and message clear to my Twitter audience? Take a look at your bio--does it align with what you want others to know about you and your business? Does it have too much business jargon or too little? It's easy to get caught up worrying about what to tweet, but take a few minutes to create a Twitter bio that is unique for you. You can change your Twitter as many times as you need in the beginning but once you find one that clearly communicates your message, stick with it to build your brand!

2. Do your tweets showcase what area of expertise you represent? People will determine whether or not to follow you by looking at your first 1-5 tweets. Do your tweets educate the Twitter community about the value you can offer? Make sure followers get a clear idea of what kinds of content you will share by pinning a Tweet to the top. Changing it frequently will continue to pique the interest of your followers.

3. Do you engage and build relationships consistently? This is the most time consuming part of the journey. Building relationships can take a few weeks or a few months. It's determined by how much you interact meaningfully on Twitter. If you're only on Twitter once every few days, your brand will take longer to stick and people will not take you seriously. You should engage 15-30 minutes once a day to grow your brand awareness, build valuable relationships, and create a valuable and engaging Twitter community that will amplify your brand.

4. Are you creating a Twitter experience worth sharing? Tweeting can be boring, lonely, and quite frankly a waste of time if no one is taking the time to read what you tweeted. Your brand will not grow, because no will care about who you are and the message you're trying to share. Use Twitter to deliver an effective and consistent experience that your audience will want to share, retweet, and like. Twitter is creating features that can help with this process. Use gifs to say hello, upload a 140 second video welcoming your new Twitter follower or use it to answer questions. Livestream to your Twitter community using Periscope. Twitter even has polls that you can create. Get creative!
Think of building your brand on Twitter in stages and try to determine where you are on this path. Once you've figured out where you are, keep tweeting, stay consistent, and build a brand worth tweeting.

Stay on the Cutting Edge

Taneka Badie

Your brand is what makes your company unique, right? It's more than the visual appearance. Although consistent marketing material is an important element to your brand, it's not the only factor. How do customers recognize your brand from others? Does your brand give them a certain emotion? Your brand is the voice of your company. Without a voice how will customers hear you in such a noisy marketplace? A successful brand focuses on their message, their customers' wants/needs, and staying on the cutting edge.

How can you get your brand message out to the audience? You must distribute unique content and visuals that represent your message. You will have to persuade and motivate your potential customers to buy your products/services. They usually don't buy from you the first time they see your brand; you will have to keep putting the message out in different ways and eventually they will buy. Here are several ways to do this:

- Distribute content on your blog
- Share it on social media platforms
- Use popular industry keywords in your posts
- Create videos and market them

Customers are the key to having a successful brand. They should always feel like they are important. Once you give the customers what they want it will create a positive experience. Satisfied customers lead to more referrals and sales. Here are a few questions you should keep in mind: What do customers like/dislike about your brand? Where do they think your brand can use improvements? What other brands have they used similar to yours? How was their experience? Getting feedback from your customers is very beneficial because it helps potential customers have a better feeling about trusting your brand. Positive feedback should be used on your social media platforms and your website.

It's not easy to stand out from the crowd. The goal is to know your target audience and your competitors. Research what your competitors are doing to increase traffic and do it better than they are. What are your competitors spending on advertising? How are they gaining a lot of online traffic? In order to stay ahead of the game, you must know what your competitors are doing and figure out how to stay on the cutting edge. Stay current on the latest trends/technology and implement that in your branding. You can see exactly how much your competitors are spending online and how they are gaining so much online traffic by using an awesome tool called **SEM Rush**. This tool will show you how to make better decisions about marketing online to your target audience.

Be Transparent

Ires D. Alliston

Have you seen those "Behind the Scenes" or "A Day in the Life" videos that big corporations started putting out a few years back? How about the ones where they introduce you to a few people at their global headquarters and show you how they run day-to-day operations? Guess where they got that idea.

Transparency is another thing that separates big corporations from small brands. Transparency, in regard to business, is being honest and open. Now I do want to add that being transparent, being honest and open is not about divulging everything for people to know including where you buy your toilet paper (unless you really want to) but it helps establish credibility.

The truth is every relationship will vary with different people as everyone is unique and how much we share will also establish how the relationship is nurtured over time. However, businesses should see that being transparent is a way to improve service and increase customer loyalty. It's a great way to connect with their customers, readers and prospects. For the same reasons mentioned elsewhere (see my tip on Stand for Something Unique), transparency may not always do as well for big business as it does for small businesses.

Stories

Ires D. Alliston

Historically, people who are great at telling captivating stories live long, prosperous lives. The desire to be entertained is in our DNA, but a good brand story isn't just about entertaining your audience, it's about making them feel. Customers today want to fall in love with small brand. When your customers read your story, they should empathize with it. It may also create brand loyalty when your customers feel compelled to share it with all of their friends. Sharing it with their friends or word of mouth marketing is a type of marketing that is powerful, effective and that no amount of money can buy.

Now, no customer wants to hear, "I built this business because I saw that it was an untapped niche," or "I did it all for the money." Also, no customer wants to read a brand's story that reads like a resume – this goes for artists and musicians as well! The most successful small brands have a story behind why they started their business that will immediately resonate with their audience. By having a story that speaks only to your audience, you are essentially filtering out a lot of unwanted leads signing up for your email list.

When writing your brand's story, use exciting, passionate adjectives. Make it pop, sizzle, ignite, so that your reader can feel your passion for what you do. A reader should be inspired by your story. They might not buy something from you the minute they finish reading your story, but they will certainly remember it. A brand's story plants the seed that will eventually grow into an orchard of customers loyal to your brand.

Creating a Good "User Experience" for Your Website

Taneka Badie

The user experience is an important element to your brand. Your website must be user-friendly and responsive because most people view their websites on their cell phones. Please keep in mind that Google will penalize websites that are not responsive which means you can miss out on a lot of online traffic. You can test your website by visiting **Google Mobile-Friendly Test**.

You can view how your website looks on different devices with a free tool called **mobiletest.me**

It is important to stay up-to-date with the ever-changing world of technology. If you don't want to lose potential customers, you must be able to grab the users' attention within seconds. The attention span of users is getting shorter by the second. If the speed of your website is not fast enough, they will be gone before it even comes up on their screens. Do you want to make your website fast on all devices? If so, start by using **Google PageSpeed Insights** to check for errors that are slowing the speed down.

Is your website functioning properly? You can perform an audit on your website for the following things:

- Broken Links
- Duplicate content
- Missing title tags
- Missing alt tags
- Missing meta description and much more.

You can try out the **SEMRush** tool for free to see what issues need to be resolved in order to gain the traffic your business deserves.

Would you be interested in knowing what your users like/dislike about your website without even asking them? Heat maps show you what areas of your website users are interested in clicking on and where they fall off. This helps with understanding their behaviors so you can improve the user experience. You can install **SumoMe** on your website to give it a try.

Make sure there are great visuals that coincide with your products/services. Never use too much content because most people will not read it. You must be easy on the eye. You can break up the content by using bullet points, lists, and visuals to represent the message you are trying to convey. A great way to keep users on your website for a longer period of time is to use videos. This helps with increasing your search rankings and reducing your bounce rates.

Being the Real Deal

JoBeth Martin

I am inviting you to take a few minutes to imagine something. Think about the person that you are when you are being your true self; functioning in your gifting, unafraid of failure and dreaming big dreams. Can you picture it?

Let's bring it to life. Picture what you are wearing. What are you doing? How are people responding in a positive way to you? How do you feel in that moment? Is your heart full and your confidence high?

I was asked to do this exercise at a conference recently and it truly impacted me. In case you are struggling to form a picture I will be vulnerable a bit and share what mine looked like.

I was standing on the stage of a conference hall filled with women there to learn how to be their best self in business and life. They were excited and expectant about I would share. Dressed in a striking blue dress that highlighted the blue in my eyes I was the picture of confidence and vibrant health. I spoke with joy, enthusiasm, wisdom and authority that inspired these women to believe in their God-given design and to walk in freedom. It was awesome!

Your picture will look completely different from mine but there is a picture that is you. Remember the last time you felt really good about what you were doing? Were you excited and fulfilled? Were you serving, organizing a task or people, working quietly by yourself or alongside of a team? What gifting, skill or personality trait was most prominent when you felt really alive and were accomplishing great and meaningful things? That is the person you were created to be!

What if you can't remember that person or have never seen yourself in that way? Then please take the time to find that person. Take time to dream, listen to your heart and write down what is really important to you. Picture how your particular strengths could play into a business.

What I discovered that day is that in personal and ministry situations I was usually myself, but in business I often had not lived up to my potential. There are many reasons this happens. Sometimes our learning curve is hard and our journey filled with difficult situations that are molding us into the person God created us to be. During these seasons we may have a difficult time walking in our potential. Often we allow the difficulties to define us and we forget the bigger picture of who we really are in our fullness.

I made a decision that day to remember and live up to my picture. I would step out in faith and take the risk of putting my true self out there. I would believe in myself and let only God define who I am. I would seek out opportunities in business just as I had in personal life and ministry to be my true authentic self. I would stand tall and be that person. Why would I want to be anyone else?

A more important question is, why would you? Why would you be willing to be anything less in life and business than your own personal best self? If you don't know who that is I would entreat you to take the time to discover it. The business world needs what you have to offer. Imagine your picture of your true self in your mind, then go for it!!

Be The Real Deal!!!

Stand for Something Unique

Ires D. Alliston

Part of humanizing your brand is coming up with a set of core values. A brand's values are much like their mission statement in that they should drive everything that you do. From every single blog post to launching a new product, a brand lives and dies by its core values.

Incidentally, this seems to be what separates the big corporations from small brands. Just in the last five or so years we've seen major corporations try to use the same formula that successful small brands have been using for ages. The reason this doesn't work for them is because people already know about Coca-Cola or what Pepsi is, for example and they will choose their preference every single time.

Although you have the CEOs from other major corporations appearing in television commercials trying desperately to humanize their brand, these methods have proven unsuccessful to big corporations – yet they will do wonders for your small business! Not that big corporations don't have values, but it can be challenging for customers to identify and relate with you when you have a skyscraper with your massive logo on it in five continents around the world.

Having brand values shows that your brand is much more than a company that makes awesome products or sells sweet services – it shows that you care. Your values can be pretty much anything – from partnering with a local non-profit, taking leadership roles in the community, prioritizing customer service and customer satisfaction, believing in humor in everything you do, or having that unique infrastructure of your business. Whatever your values are, they must be authentic and unique.

The best brands have a set of values that are all related to one another. This paints a bigger picture of what you do and why you're doing it. Don't just tell your audience that believe in something; explain how you feel about the issue and what you are doing to fix it. Your brand might make the best faux-leather boots in the world, for example, but when you explain that you're only making them to stop animal abuse, the big picture will make a lot more sense to your audience.

Let Your Light Shine

Carol D. Neal

My business partner, Tracee Randall, talks elsewhere in this section about how important it is to brand YOU, not just your business or the company you represent. That is why her website is www.TraceeRandall.com. But another way to brand yourself is to create an "umbrella" that represents you well and is flexible enough to incorporate almost any business you would embrace...because people do change focus from time to time. That is what I have done with my brand, Let Your Light Shine.

At the time I chose it I was a PartyLite Consultant. The words obviously were very appropriate for the company, which sells candles and related accessories. But more importantly, they represented ME. I have a passion to help others let their own lights shine, by helping them step out of their comfort zones to share their faith and to share their gifts. I want to inspire others by taking these actions myself so I can "light a way out of the darkness" for someone else. I love to connect people, to give them opportunities to succeed, and to provide resources for their personal growth. It all made sense.

But as much as I loved the PartyLite products, after 6 years I knew I didn't want to spend the rest of my life carting them around to shows at peoples' homes, and that was about the time I met Tracee and was introduced to Reliv International. Reliv is a company known for health and nutrition products. Yay, my brand still worked! Now I could help you Let Your Light Shine with Energy and Clarity! And when I added Organo's healthy coffees and teas as another income stream, I could help you Let Your Light Shine with Health and Prosperity.

I created other tag lines for myself to reinforce MY brand with everything I represent. Let Your Light Shine in your Career and Community (Credit Professionals International). Let Your Light Shine in your Business and Networking (Atlanta Business Spotlight). Let Your

Light Shine in all your Connections (Xperience Connections). You get the idea. No matter where life takes me in the future, people will always understand my purposes and goals and associate me with Let Your Light Shine if I stay true to myself and to this brand.

Two of our new Xperience Connections Leaders have recently used this same concept. Nadia Torabi, XC Acworth/Dallas, has embraced "Nadia's Garden" to include several different companies that people can "pick" products from...and JoBeth Martin, XC Kennesaw/Town Center, (who is also one of the other authors in this book) makes sure that everything she does is in alignment with her core beliefs as "Righteous Oaks". What speaks to you? More importantly, what do you want to come to mind when other people think of you? THAT is your brand!

Bad Branding Habits

Taneka Badie

As a business owner you should put out a professional image that represents what your brand stands for. Don't make it a habit to throw things together just because you need marketing materials to promote your business. You may not have a clue how the design process works so always ask questions to get a better understanding. This helps when you decide to hire a professional.

Here are some common mistakes business owners make:

1) **Find designers that are cheaper**

    I have had potential clients not want to work with me because they thought my prices were too high so they went with someone cheaper. Once they received the work they were either not satisfied with the outcome, or the work couldn't be used due to the quality. So they came back to me to fix it. They got what they paid for. If you want customers to invest in your brand you must be willing to invest in it first. If you want your business to grow, a professional brand image is essential to your business.

2) **Not using a consistent look & feel**

    Often times, I see brands using Vista print business card templates and a different look on their marketing material/website. They also use too many different fonts within their brand. Everything looks cluttered and unorganized. This confuses the audience.

3) **Your brand shouldn't reflect things you like personally if it's not related**

    Just because your favorite color is pink and you like butterflies doesn't mean it should be incorporated into your branding. Don't take it too personal. Don't just go with the first idea you get. Developing a clever brand takes time and research. You definitely don't want potential customers to mistake your brand for another one due to similar identities.

If you don't have a budget to hire a designer, you could download free design assets from **Creative Market** which includes: graphics, stock photos, templates, website themes and much more. You can also use **Skillshare** which is a subscription based online learning community to learn basic skills in design.

Now that you understand the common mistakes, it's time to fix them. This may be hindering your brand from gaining new customers.

Gain the World Without Losing Your Soul

JoBeth Martin

What a great example of practical wisdom for us to follow in business. We live in a society that has changed a great deal in the last 20 years. What used to be the norm of right and wrong has changed. If we are not careful we will change with it and not even realize what has happened. Sadly, in many ways society no longer has absolutes. With this void in society it is important that we as individuals make our own choices about what we will believe concerning right and wrong. Integrity is an individual choice and perhaps it means a great deal more because of the personal necessity to choose.

For a minute let's think about how choice and integrity play into our brand. What does your personal brand look like? What does it stand for? What is it selling? How does it feel? With our brand we get to choose everything from the colors that we use and the atmosphere that they project. We think about the name of our company, the impression that our website makes and even the font that we use in our printed material. As entrepreneurs we truly have a choice to brand ourselves as we like.

This is just one reason to be an entrepreneur and own our own business. We then have the choice to decide how our brand is presented to the world. We get to choose integrity. We get to decide with great thought how we will make our mark on the world and what we represent as we present ourselves.

However, many of us as entrepreneurs are also associated with companies as independent partners. As employees or even independent distributors we would be wise to choose the company that we align ourselves with because we agree with their culture and branding. But what happens if the management goes a different direction and loses their way? Then we are left defending something we don't agree with and can't change. How do we control our impact and reputation on the world in this case? Can we prevent that from happening?

First, choose wisely who you will align yourself with as a partner. Look closely at the company to see what they are made of and how their founders and leaders operate. Do they have a reputation of honesty and caring? Do they have a record of questionable activity? Do they make unreasonable promises of an easy fortune? What is most important to them? Is their mission to make a positive impact or just to make money? One of the things that drew me to one of the companies that I have partnered with, Nerium, is that their mission statement is to "Make People Better." Over time I have watched carefully and discovered that they really make this a priority.

In addition to choosing wisely to associate with a company that you can be proud of, you can also make it a priority to brand yourself first and foremost. In other words, choose to brand yourself even more than you brand your company. Companies may come and go but you and your reputation will last a lifetime. Let the company play a supporting role to you; not the other way around. Work hard to know who you are and what you have to offer the world.

You are your brand. Everything you are and do in business tells the world who you are and what you are made of so be sure that the message you put out there is exactly what you want the world to read. Be sure that you do not GAIN THE WHOLE WORLD AND LOSE YOUR OWN SOUL.

The Logo

Ires D. Alliston

Having the right brand logo is one of the most underrated components of a successful brand. Sure, you might have a cute way you spell your company's name, but the perfect logo makes the perfect brand. It should also look natural when paired together with your brand's name, font and colors.

This can be either very difficult or very expensive sometimes, and finding the right logo to represent your company can be a painstaking task. Once you decide on a logo, switching it up a few years into your business will confuse people and may even cost you customers. Make a bold decision when it comes to your logo at the very beginning and stick with it.

That doesn't mean that you'll be stuck with the same logo you decide on today in ten years from now. Look at how Instagram recently *evolved* with their logo, just like they are currently evolving their brand with a new algorithm. Think about what you want to use your logo for in the future. Will it be a watermark on every original photo you take? Will it come to life and wink at the audience in videos you create? Think beyond simple business cards and Gravatar. The possibilities are only limited by your imagination.

A logo should not only represent your brand's core values, but it should also represent your ideal customer, as well. The first place to look for inspiration when you're developing your brand's logo is at the logos your competitors are using. Pick them apart and analyze them. Are they characters? Are they symbols? What colors do they use? How are their customers reacting to their logo? If their customers are not reacting to your competition's logo; that tells you to do the opposite of whatever they're doing. If your competition's customers like the character in their logo, come up with your own even more lovable character.

I recommend you come up with 3-5 different logos or design variations and do a focus group on Facebook or an industry forum before you launch. You can even go as far as create a content by sharing your design with companies like 99designs. They have design contests with their community of more than a million international designers. A little peer feedback can go a long way. When you find the logo that makes people feel like something fun and exciting is about to happen whenever they see it, you know you have found *"the one"*.

Brand YOU

Tracee Randall

If I could look back over my experience in building several successful brick and mortar businesses as well as a couple of profitable direct sales companies, the one thing that I would have done sooner is *brand* myself. Let's make it clear that I am not a branding expert, however, over the past couple of years I have realized the importance of branding *ME* first, and the company/companies I represent second.

In the world we live in today, social media and the internet have made getting our message out there very easy—there are tips shared in this book about the power of videos, using platforms such as Twitter, LinkedIn, Facebook and more to expose your business to the world. There have been overnight success stories from Facebook videos that have catapulted people who are virtually unknown to internet fame, which has resulted in big profits! The biggest mistake I see entrepreneurs make, and especially people in the direct sales industry, is they brand the company, but never take the time to brand themselves.

Of course we want to be "product and company loyal", but the true foundation of *YOUR* business is **YOU**. One of my mentors in the DS industry shared this with us and it was one of those "AHA" moments. He drew a sketch of a triangle and explained that this is the strongest of all the geometric shapes. Then he pointed to the base—"This," he said, "is the strongest part of the triangle, the foundation, the base, and therefore the most important part of the structure." He asked us what we believed to be the most important part of our business/direct sales company, and the answers varied from "product", "leadership" to "industry". He smiled wisely and shook his head, "No, the most important part of your business is YOU. YOU are the foundation." He was teaching on working on ourselves first, our mindset, our product knowledge, our work ethics, our integrity, our persistence and consistency, but he also was very straightforward with us. Companies come and go. Industry trends change. Leadership changes, compensation plans change. The company that we are so enamored by today, the products that we love, the leadership that we follow—all of these things can be gone tomorrow, but YOU are the common denominator, you are the reason people choose to use your product, YOU are the reason people decide to partner with you in the business!

I have seen too many incredible people talk incessantly about their company, BRAND their company and then within 1-2 years something changes and they switch companies and they have to start all over again. Unless the person is very strong, it is difficult for them to "come back" from the change and they spend way too much time explaining why they left the first company and now the "best thing since sliced bread" is this new endeavor.

This testimony forced me into immediate action, and I hope it will do the same for you. Susan had started her career in the direct sales industry and saw immediate financial success. She catapulted quickly and wrote a book about the process—it too became widely read and she had created another significant income stream. She became widely known for her business training and coaching. Her company grew, her NAME grew and she branded herself and became her own company. It was time to create her website, and since the name of her company was HER NAME, she went online to purchase it. She was stunned to find that her name had already been purchased and was "for sale" for $10K!! She contacted the owners and through some investigation found that a savvy business person had realized before she did how powerful she had become, and she was forced to pay that person $10K to get her website! What should have cost a couple of bucks cost her big money! So the "insider tip" that I am sharing here is this: whether you are just starting out or have been working your business for a while, whether you're ready to build your own website or NOT, go ahead and buy your domain name. A domain name will range from 99 cents upward, but is well-worth the investment. People will forget the name of your company and the products you endorse, BUT they never forget YOUR NAME! BUY YOUR NAME—I have owned several companies over the past 10 years, but my name has never changed! Brand YOU!

TIPS ON NETWORKING

"The richest people in the world look for and build networks. Everyone else looks for work."

~ Robert Kiyosaki

Plan Ahead to Follow-Up

Carol D. Neal

Here are two more steps you can do in advance of your next meeting or event to ensure you have a successful networking experience and set yourself up for effective follow-up.

First, always do your homework on the meeting itself. Find out the format...how much time will you have to share, do they encourage passing of business cards and flyers, is there a cost, is there a meal, what is the timeline? If the event listing does not provide all of this information, reach out to the organizer or an existing member and ask. You may be surprised at how eager they will be to help you and answer your questions, AND you'll have created an opportunity to thank them in person when you meet them at the event. As an event organizer myself I always appreciate it when people ask in advance. And you don't do yourself any favors by saying at a meeting "I'm sorry, I didn't know if I should bring business cards or not", or "I wasn't sure how much time I got to speak" or worse yet, "I didn't know I'd be asked to speak". You're at a networking meeting...ALWAYS be prepared to speak if given the opportunity. Admitting that you aren't prepared for the meeting will leave the impression that you aren't prepared to do business. If you can't find out the details, prepare for anything and everything to the best of your ability! Have several intro's ready...from 30 seconds to 3 minutes...and always take business cards and writing materials with you. Also be sure you know exactly where the meeting is and how to get there AND how long it will take...a little advance planning here can save you a lot of embarrassment and missed opportunity! Be sure you have the address and organizer's contact number with you just in case.

Second, we all hear it...the fortune is in the follow-up. What most people don't realize is that effective follow-up starts BEFORE the meeting even begins. Always schedule your follow-up in advance. This is a simple step that most people miss that can make a HUGE difference in your success. At the same time you put a networking event on your calendar, mark time on your calendar to follow-up from that specific event. It might be 20-30 minutes within the next 48 hours, or it could be that you set aside a couple hours one or two days each week to do follow-up and you want to enter the name of the event in your next scheduled session. Too often we flit from meeting to meeting and, because we don't have a set follow-up time SCHEDULED for that meeting, we let life happen and two days become five and then a week and 2 weeks later we realize we never made the connections we promised...and in the meantime we've met a hundred other people and don't even remember the people we wanted to connect with from the first meeting. Then a couple more weeks go by and we feel it's too late to reach out. If you will SCHEDULE TIME ON YOUR CALENDAR FOR THE FOLLOW-UP at the same time you schedule the event itself, you will be much more likely to get it done in a timely manner, and you will definitely reap the results! The actual follow-up consists of making the referrals and connections you promised people happen as well as entering new people you've met into your automated or manual follow-up system and reaching out to the people you wanted to connect with yourself.

You MUST have a consistent system to be able to follow-up consistently! At Atlanta Business Spotlight we have found two that, combined, meet all of our needs. We use the automated card-reader and customizable campaign system from LeadOutcome to manage our data base and email campaigns, and we use SendOutCards for our regular mail campaigns and for all occasions that require a more personal touch. This combination works for us, especially the automated card reader, because it only takes a few seconds to capture all the information we need...no more boxes of business cards to wade through! And we can actually have a campaign ready to go specific to the meeting before we get there, so all we do is take a picture of the business cards we've collected and we're done...the campaign is off and running! If you are interested in learning more about either of these services, let me know. But whatever you do, find some sort of system, even a manual one, that works for you and implement it by scheduling that time on your calendar to follow through on your follow-up!

The Quick Connection #1: Differentiate!

Bonnie Ross-Parker

Maybe you're a veteran of the networking arena and agree you could be more effective. Or, perhaps, you're just getting started and would like to better understand how to network productively. "The Quick Connection" in 3 parts is a reference tool to help you effectively impact others and increase your success.

Here's the familiar scenario: Show up. Shake as many hands as possible. Give out and get as many business cards as you can. Tell everyone, "I'll call you" or expect the people you meet to actually call you! Consider a better approach. **Strategy #1 – Differentiate**. Being unique distinguishes you from others, especially those in the same industry. Remember when you were young and fitting in meant doing the same thing as everyone else in your peer group? Being the same was a way of establishing acceptance. In business, the opposite is true. It's an advantage when you differ. For example, initiate conversations with people *you don't know*. Ask how he/she got into the industry they're in, what trends they anticipate or what they did before their current career. Ask what they find is their biggest challenge. If you're wondering why I suggest this line of questioning, it's because most business people are more eager to share what *they* do then to engage in building rapport with someone else. Find out what a good lead is for the individual you'd like to assist. If you want to get to know another business person, consider extending an invitation to an upcoming networking event as your guest. When you implement this strategy, the emphasis is off of you and focused elsewhere. This is not typical in networking situations.

Please do not indiscriminately hand out your business card. That is indicative of individuals eager to sell instead of to listen and learn.

Consider asking for business cards only from those connections with whom you want to follow up. That decision alone puts you in the driver's seat, let's you make the next move and places you in a position to stand out separate from anyone else.

When you differentiate yourself in a crowded marketplace, you have clearly demonstrated that you are the person with whom others who will want to do business. Give this one strategy your best effort!

The Quick Connection #2: Be Memorable

Bonnie Ross-Parker

In The Quick Connection Collection, **Strategy # 2: Be Memorable**, learning how to stand out is another way to differentiate oneself. There are two aspects to this strategy. They are: being remembered for your appearance and being remembered because of your behavior. And, regarding both aspects, it's easy to realize you can be remembered for the *wrong* reason(s) and for the *right* one(s)! Of course, I'm eager for you to positively represent yourself in order to create the most credibility and the most effective results.

There is no doubt you and I have both been in networking situations where the appearance of some participants has left us knowing we'd unlikely engage either in conversation or in client engagement/referrals. Believe me, this has nothing to do with judgment. This is strictly the realization that professional indicators of pride and appearance have a lot to do with being serious about wanting to do business. Individuals who care about the way they look, how they show up and present themselves are likely to also deal with business in a confident and businesslike manner.

We all know what dressing appropriately means. I'm suggesting to step up one's appearance a notch so how you dress stands out from the crowd. It can be the choice of consistent color, a unique style or anything that others will notice reflects you! Think of famous musical/theatrical individuals who have their own easy recognizable style! That's what I'm suggesting you consider! (For me, I always wear cowboy boots! No exception, ever!)

Moving on, let's address behavior as another critical factor for you to consider as you network or in life for that matter. Examples include: Honor your commitments. Do what you say you're going to do. Pay the bill when you invite someone for coffee/lunch. Follow up in a timely fashion. Do more listening and less talking. Share and care instead of tell and sell. ANYTHING you can do that reflects positive behavior will definitely separate you from those who are less than professional. You are in the driver's seat. What you say, what you do and how you interface with others is critical to being effective in both business and life. You decide how YOU want to be remembered!

The Quick Connection #3: Make A Difference

Bonnie Ross-Parker

In the Quick Connection Collection, **Strategy #3 is Make A Difference.** It's a fact that when asked, most individuals will say that they want to be known or recognized that their life mattered because who they are made a difference. When all is said and done, how we conduct ourselves, appreciate, share, support and care about others are all strong indicators of how we choose to live our lives. A life well lived is focused on service, generosity and integrity.

You simply never know who you will meet and the difference you can make in someone else's life or the difference an encounter will make in your life. Replace a simply thank you with "I appreciate you". Go out of your way to make a newcomer feel comfortable at a networking event. Introduce people you know to people they need to meet. Introduce people you meet to people they need to know.

Gestures don't have to be big. They just have to be sincere. It's important to note that how you do anything is how you do everything. Once you are mindful about the way you are interacting with others, you start to quickly recognize ways to make a difference. This is not unlike 'pay it forward' with the intention of choosing to be at your best.

Several years ago I accepted a no-fee speaking engagement. I chose to help out a young woman who was looking for a speaker for an upcoming monthly meeting that had a last minute cancellation. While it would not have been my first choice to 'fill in' for 'free', I had a feeling it might lead to something at another time. I delivered my best (as if I was actually paid), graciously accepted the praise and appreciation and was told afterward, "I hope someday I can return the favor."

Months later I received a call from the same gal who had asked me to speak on networking. It seems she had received a call to give her best referral for someone to speak on networking at a women's conference in Nuremberg, Germany! Guess who landed her first (and only) international engagement? You, too, can choose to make a difference and experience what happens.

Build Better Relationships Through Volunteering

Laura B. Baker

The size of the networking group does not matter. Every group needs help to provide a successful meeting, conference, or organization. There is always something to do.

When I first joined the Georgia Real Estate Investors Association, it was the largest group in the nation. I went to the monthly meeting and had no clue where to start. Who do you talk to first? How do you know who to meet and get acquainted with? Who can you trust?

Volunteering to help gets the attention of the people in charge. Whether you are helping carry boxes in from the car or answering phones in the office, people can always use a helping hand. You have many talents that can be used to help. The more time you spend helping out, the more people you meet. The more people you meet, the more you learn. The more you learn, the better you will be able to make wise decisions, which was why you joined the group in the first place.

You joined to meet "like-minded" people, and the BEST way to get to know people is to work side by side. The knowledgeable people and the people who run the group have a common interest with you. The information you learn while working with them is much better than anything you can pay to learn in a seminar or class. Plus, you are building relationships with people who can help you.

Imagine calling someone you have never met with an important question. What kind of answer would you expect to get? Professional, of course, but not personal. Now imagine you are calling the same person, but you had just spent an afternoon working on a project together. What kind of answer would you expect this time? Do you think the quality of the answer would be different? Because you worked together, their answer will be more personal and detailed than they would give to someone they don't know. You've invested in something important to them; they will be more willing to invest in you.

Volunteering allows you the opportunity to develop relationships with knowledgeable and highly skilled people who are more willing to share their knowledge with you because you took the time to lend a helping hand.

Your Network = Your Net Worth

Deborah Daniel

Networking is a key strategy in my marketing toolkit. It is certainly not the only marketing I do for my business but is possibly the most profitable—and not from only a financial sense. I have three major goals when I am networking: to gain access to more potential clients, inform others what I do and find resources for my business.

In networking I don't focus on trying to find an instant customer at an event, remember we network to *tell* not sell! I am looking for referral partners that have a complimentary service that is already working with my ideal clients. Developing these kinds of relationships instead of looking for an individual in the room that may be a customer will pay off with huge dividends over time. By nurturing these referral partner relationships you put the whole "Know, Like and Trust" system on steroids. The steady stream of warm leads you will receive from these referral partners far outweighs any effort you can put into networking for individual customers.

You need to spend quality time crafting your message of what you will tell people at networking events. Focus on the problem that you solve so it is easy for someone you are talking with to think of someone who might need that type of help. One strategy for telling what you do is to network with a buddy. Sometimes it is a lot easier to build each other up to the people you are networking with than to tell about yourself. When it comes from you— it sounds like bragging. When it comes from someone else it is an endorsement.

Some of the best connections I have made while networking were actually resources for my business and personal development. I met my business coach, became part of a mastermind group and have made many friends while networking. The added benefit of pursuing the art of "Know, Like and Trust" is that those people that you meet that have this same philosophy really connect with you outside of business as well.

It often turns out that you have a lot besides business in common with the people that you meet at networking events.

Developing a network that is a reliable supply of clients, vendors and friendships takes time, but just like building your business and your fortune there is a cumulative effect of your actions. The more you network, the more people you meet and the deeper connections you develop the bigger your business, influence and ultimately your fortunes will be! So get out there and build your network and watch your net worth climb!

The Power of Collaboration

Corey Moore

It takes a village... Two heads are better than one... Potluck dinners... Carpooling... Strength in numbers... These are all terms that we have heard of and understand. Their concept is simple, two or more is better than one. When there are difficult tasks that need to accomplished, these terms all state that the problem gets easier based on how many people are involved in its solution.

Business is one of the hardest 'tasks' that I have ever been involved in. But, for whatever reason, when most people start a business, especially solo-preneurs (not having a business partner), this concept is soon forgotten. Business owners walk out into the world every day and go into battle. Each day is filled with ups and downs, problems and solutions, accomplishment and failures. If this is the nature of business, why don't we apply the same basic concept of 2 is better than 1? If we all agree that having others around us for support is a lot easier than doing it by ourselves, then why isn't that our strategy from the very beginning?

Every project that I do, I challenge myself to collaborate. I first figure out what I want to accomplish. I then figure out who and what I will need to accomplish it. When I have a firm grasp on the elements needed, I then try to find others who are also looking for the same elements to accomplish their projects. If we are both working together to acquire the same elements, it is just like carpooling. Since we are both going in the same direction, why not save money, time, and other resources by metaphorically getting in one car and traveling together?

How do I find people I can carpool with? Networking! Every time I go to a networking event, if I find a client, great, but I look for other things. We have a concept called the 3 C's of networking: A Client, A Collaborator, A Competitor. These are the three things a person should be on the lookout for when they go to a networking event. Since a client is harder to find, I spend more time focused on looking for collaborators and competitors. Their clients probably look just like mine. If that is the case, they need the same elements that I do to attract them. Why not work together?

I can testify that I am in the position that I am in today by collaborating. There were many projects that I overcame that, very simply, I could not have tackled by myself. Business, in general, is very hard. You always have to be on the lookout for things that can make it easier. Let collaboration be your next weapon of choice before you leave the house for battle.

My "Stalking" Secret

Carol D. Neal

Have a goal in mind for every networking meeting you attend. Elsewhere in this book you'll read about the importance of mindset and affirmations, and about learning to give before you seek to receive. When I first started attending networking meetings I would go in with goals like "I'm going to sell to two people today" or "I'm going to meet three people who I can add to my team". While it was great to give myself a goal, walking into a meeting with THAT type of mindset ensured that I repelled more people than I attracted. It was obvious that I was trying to move every conversation into a sale.

Over the years I've learned to change that around so that my meeting goals are based on creating relationships for long-term results, instead of trying to immediately put money in my pocket. That means I attend every meeting with an eye to helping others first. So now my goal may be "I'm going to find at least two people today for whom I can find great connections." Then I LISTEN when people give their referral requests and I WRITE DOWN one or two people that I could connect them with. I ASK questions about resources they might need and projects they are doing so I can think of more people. Then at the end of the meeting I TELL them who I'm going to connect them with, and then after the meeting I DO it.

A great way to make sure you succeed at connecting is to identify ahead of time some of the people you particularly want to meet at the event. You can ask the organizer who they feel would be a good collaborator or referral partner for you, or reach out to someone who has been to the group before and ask them who they recommend you meet. If the meeting is online on Facebook or Meetup, take a look at some of the people who have RSVP'd...what companies or products do they represent? Arc they members of other groups? Do they have similar hobbies or interests you can talk to them about? Is this a person with a circle of influence you would like to enter?

Taking a few extra moments to select and "study" a few people ahead of time will make the most of the time you spend at the meeting. I'm really not advocating cyber-stalking, just suggesting you do some due diligence to determine who might be the best people to connect with at that meeting, and then seeing how you can be of service to them. And it's a great ice-breaker when you can walk up to someone and say "Ralph, I'm so glad to meet you. Joe X. said I should be sure and introduce myself because....." Or "Betty, I was so excited to see that you were going to be at this meeting. I have been interested in learning more about XYZ and I understand that you are an expert in that field." Or "John, I'm so glad to meet you. I noticed online that you are a member of the ABC group. I've been thinking about attending some of their meetings. Do you recommend them?"

Being able to share a little something about a few key people in advance will also go a long way when you are introducing them to other people, help you stand out as a "go to" person, and make it easier for you to find those people you want to connect.

An important point here is to always be sincere. Please do not feign interest in someone's stamp collecting or spin class just to get to know them if those activities don't interest you. Find the common ground, and build upon it!

Be in the Moment, and Be You!

Stephanie Combes

Every person has made a commitment to something that they have dreaded to attend. The most important trait to have is the motivation to just go. You never know when you are going to meet the next person who is going to change your life. You never know when you are going to form that connection that enhances your idea. You must go into every room as if you are transparent. You must be yourself and the right people will gravitate towards you and make your business venture more poignant and your life feel more valuable.

We have all worked for companies that have seemed to drain the soul right out of our smiles. Those companies still make up our resumes and they still provide us with experience that is necessary for our success in our next business triumph or tragedy. Removing one brick from a structure won't make a house crumble. One burnt cookie in a batch won't change a person's love of cookies. Carry these thoughts with you, and adopt them as a part of you

Do what you gotta do, as long as you're doing *you*! I found myself in a company that threw out most of my innovative ideas because they weren't ready for them, and it was easy to second guess my ability and worth. The job quickly took the life out of me and challenged my identity. If you are doing things that don't reflect who you are, then you aren't doing what you were intended to do. You have the freedom to make every decision that is right for your person and be vocal about it. This is what has shaped me into the person that many companies now want on their team. We have been taught all our lives to roll with the punches. Now is your chance to take those punches and turn them into something that YOU can be proud of. The magic is within yourself. That is the biggest tip of all.

Some Will, Some Won't, Someone is Waiting!

Deborah Daniel

Being authentic in business is mission critical to success. You have to know what you stand for, know the value you bring to your customers and stand by that. While you can have different messages of what you do for different audiences there cannot be different versions of who you are as the core of the business. This authenticity also gives you the ability to put yourself and your business out there over and over again in networking situations.

You can be the best accountant, attorney, hair stylist or landscaper or even have the very best products, but if no one knows about you—you will not be selling a lot of what you have to offer. Your role as an entrepreneur is to make sure enough people know what you do to keep the revenue flowing. Sometimes this means some rejection and this is hard for some people—but then again networking and entrepreneurship are not for the faint of heart.

You can't be afraid of NO. When a prospect says no to you in regards to a sale or even another meeting to find out if you can work together—you can't take it personally. It is your job as the entrepreneur to spend your time on revenue generating activities—do the sales conversations, do the networking, and do the follow-up. If you make enough connections, and have enough opportunities to present yourself and your services, the sales will come.

Remember— "no" does not always mean no forever—it could just be no for now. People buy or don't but for too many reasons to even think about. If you keep connecting and keep meeting new people some of those people will do business with you. So when someone says no, remember when it comes to buying from you—some will, some won't but someone is waiting to be your next potential customer!

The Meeting After the Meeting

Laura B. Baker

There is no denying I am a strong advocate of the volunteer system. Too many doors have been opened for me with a handshake and job well done, to refute this conclusion. It is by far the easiest way to the fast track and the inner circle.

It is also the best way to get the invitation to my favorite networking activity. Most every meeting that I have attended, no matter if it was weekly, monthly, or annually, has included what I like to call "the meeting-after-the-meeting." This is where those *in the know* or group leaders go out for food, relaxation, celebration, and networking after the event has concluded. These folks work hard, are still energized and are ready to release that energy. There is a certain power in that momentum. Harnessed and focused with a group of like-minded people all positive energy is shared and dispersed among the folks there.

The meeting-after-the-meeting is for those who are serious about their commitment to the project at hand. When others have long gone home to their cozy beds, the real business, the real work is done there. How do you get invited to the meeting-after-the-meeting? You ASK. You volunteer, you stay late and become a part of the meeting rather than just a spectator.

Gloves and pretense are removed, the conversation is peeled down to personal experience, and there is a genuine openness and camaraderie. You are among friends and friends share freely. The truly wise incorporate this into their way of thinking and use it to navigate through the obstacles. The learning curve can be shortened by years with this strategy alone.

Another benefit would be the personal relationships. It makes a tremendous difference when you call someone and they know you already. Just imagine how differently the conversation would go if you had to get acquainted right then, versus you having had dinner with them a few nights before. They already have a vested interest in you. It is much simpler to accomplish your goals when talking to your new *friend* rather than a complete stranger. Those who stay for the meeting-after-the-meeting are the movers and shakers, they are the decision-makers, they are the ones you want to learn from!

I know, in my own experience, I was able to meet more leaders and people of prominence simply by going to the meeting-after-the-meeting. By using this one technique, I was able to meet Presidents, CEO's, and other people of influence I never would have been able to meet otherwise. *Now* each one knows *me* and how I roll. They don't play dodge ball when I need to get in touch with them. And on that rare occasion when I need something, they are much more willing to step in and help.

This strategy really comes in handy when you are trying to build a team of experts. I know as the Director of Education for GaREIA it was an invaluable tool. I was able to really get to know the local and national experts and it allowed me a way to vet the speakers and instructors for many of our programs.

This is the best way to the "Fast Track"—your way to the real perks and relationships that you are networking for in the first place.

Always Give More Than You Take-You Reap What You Sow

JoBeth Martin

Scripture reminds us, we reap what we sow. I believe that is true in life, relationships and business. As we think about prospecting it is obvious if we sow seeds by getting information out to a lot of people that we will eventually reap a harvest of more business because of the efforts we have put in. This is true. The more seeds that you put into the ground the more likely it will be that some will sprout and eventually you will have a larger harvest.

But I would like for us to consider a deeper meaning of reaping what we sow. I challenge you to be the individual in business who always gives more than you take. For me that was natural in relationships and ministry. I am compelled to make a difference and to see change and impact in the lives of others. So how would this translate into the business world? Is it enough just to give, to be kind, to make a difference and have impact? What about expenses, making a profit, paying the bills? Does giving more than I take accomplish those things and put money in the bank? It took me a while to answer those questions in my own heart and mind.

From the very beginning of my business I felt that it was connected to a call on my life to share truth, see people walk in freedom and in their God-given creation. So how does that fit with business? Aren't I supposed to set goals, make sales and find success? It seemed like I was double-minded. This is what I am discovering. If you always have the goal to give more than you take, you will eventually reap a harvest in relationship and in business. What does that look like?

My first suggestion is to make an effort to always be in the moment. Give the person you are with your full attention. Have at the forefront of your mind how can I assist this person and bring value to their life? It frees you up to <u>not</u> be thinking things like; I wonder if they want to buy my product or will they lead me to someone who may help my business? Of course those are legitimate questions. We all need to make sales and we all need good leads. Perhaps we can let those things be the result of good networking, not the goal. Give them your full attention and trust the goodwill to follow.

Secondly, ask yourself what is best for them? Honestly, if your product or service is really not the best thing for them at this point in their life, don't push it. Do the right thing for them. Remember the golden rule was golden for a reason. Do unto others what you would want done to you.

Lately I find myself looking at every business that comes across my path with this question in mind, "who do I know that would benefit from these products or even from this business?" Wow, what a change in thought process that has been. No, my business is not right for everyone. But maybe there is a business that is right for them and would bring tremendous blessing in their life. Be in the habit of keeping your eyes and your heart open for how you can share great businesses or products even if it does not directly impact you.

Remember if YOU REAP WHAT YOU SOW and YOU ALWAYS GIVE MORE THAN YOU TAKE...you will reap an abundant harvest!

Always Share a Story-60 Seconds to Impress

Tracee Randall

One of the biggest fears that most people have is public speaking. We've all heard that most people would rather DIE than stand up in front of people and speak! As small business owners, if we are out networking at events and meetings, there is always the possibility that we will be asked to share about our business—and most networking events allow from 30 seconds to 3 minutes to speak. In our networking workshops (#BeTheVoice Trainings), my business partner, Carol Neal and I teach small business owners that they MUST find a way to stand out from the rest of the crowd, to be *different,* to be *memorable!*

The best way we can do this is to actually *PREPARE* our 1-minute presentation in advance. Most people, because they don't like doing it, avoid the most important aspect of this part of networking—*preparing* a well-structured, impactful 1-minute presentation that will capture the attention of the attendees. What I know is that MOST of the time when others are sharing their 1-minute, the rest of the group is thinking, "what am I gonna say when it's my turn?" and not even listening to the speaker. And most of the time I think, why *should* they listen? It's usually BORING, uninteresting, repetitive information that we've heard over and over before.

I'm going to use skin care as an example. Most skin care reps say something like this, "My name is Amy and I'm with XYZ Skincare. We have a blah blah blah and a whole lotta yak yak yak that have these ingredients that do this, that and the other." They end with "I'm a good referral for ANYONE with skin," and sit down, grateful it's over.

We hear it over and over, yet we somehow forget it when we speak— "Facts tell, stories SELL". Most small business owners make the mistake of just sharing the same old facts that we all know and have heard over and over! What would YOU think if you heard something like this:

"My customer Susie was so embarrassed by her acne it caused her to stay home from school some days, and she found herself becoming introverted and afraid to meet new people. She always felt like people were staring at her acne. My name is Amy and I am with XYX Skincare. (**NOW you have people's attention—they want to learn more about Susie!**) After using our basic skincare for 7 days, Susie noticed that the redness had diminished. After 28 days of consistent use she had no acne symptoms and she began to gain confidence in her appearance. After 90 days she had seen such great results that her grades were improving, she got a part time job as a waitress and she even started dating! *I* am a ***great referral*** for your friend's daughter who is in her teens and is embarrassed about her skin!" Wow!

In 2009 I joined a formal networking group that had a "closed seat" format which meant that I was the only person who could talk about nutrition. The product that I endorsed was simple and it worked, and there was a whole lot of "science behind the product." Each week I received referrals from the group because they could identify with the stories I shared AND they could REMEMBER them!

I generated over $60,000 in PROFIT from the referrals of that networking group that year! Stories SELL. After I had been a part of the group for about 6 months, one of the members told me that the person who held the seat before me NEVER shared stories or testimonies. As a result, she generated no referrals, no new customers, and she quit networking because "it didn't work."

PREPARATION is key to your success in networking. The day before each meeting I would write my 1-minute, memorize it, and was confident the next morning—I had 60-Seconds to Impress!

Networking Without a Meeting

Laura B. Baker

Recently I was asked how to successfully network if you can't (or won't) go to meetings. Let's face it, not everyone can give up an evening or two every week. Some people are too busy with school, jobs, and family obligations, or they simply live too far from the activities. There's a plethora of reasons to keep someone away from the meetings. Even so, meeting new people is critical to your success.

What are you supposed to do if you can't get to the meetings? How do you go about building relationships? There must be an easy way to introduce yourself and meet people.

There is a solution, and it is quite simple. It doesn't even cost anything to implement. You can start where you are at, literally. The circumstances or location are not important. It is up to you when and where to use it. A simple "hi" and a smile to whoever is in your vicinity starts the ball rolling. Make a joke if you can. Not every situation lends itself to humor, but most do. Generally, people won't look at you as if you have a third eye if they are laughing with you. They will accept what you are saying as a friendly gesture because that is exactly what you are offering. Lifetime relationships can begin with a smile. It works anywhere with anyone at any time. It's called the "Three Foot Rule." All you have to do is talk to everyone who gets within three feet of you.

This is one of my favorite strategies. It affords the opportunity to talk with a great many people, opens doors that may have otherwise been closed, and it's really quite simple if talking to people comes naturally to you. As a matter of fact, the "Three Foot Rule" is one of the tools I used when I met the publishers of this book. It was several years ago, and we were able to build lifelong relationships. The blessings I have been able to receive are priceless and I continue to benefit every day.

Not everyone, however, is comfortable talking to complete strangers. Well, get over it! I apologize if this sounds harsh. People who are serious about growing and improving their plight must move out of their comfort zone. Adjust your attitude. Meeting new people is the highest priority when networking.

It will get easier the more you practice. There are as many different ways to start a conversation as there are people. Getting the conversation going is the important thing. Once you feel comfortable with the smaller conversations in everyday life, you can move on to more targeted conversations as you build your confidence. Use your best asset: You!

Success Is Not a Zero Sum Game

Deborah Daniel

I love connecting people—when I meet a person at a networking event and get an idea of what they do almost immediately I can think of two or three connections that I know will help that person's business—a possible client, a referral partner or a collaboration opportunity. If I know a connection will be beneficial for the person I am referring as well as the other person, I make the connection even if I know that the person may not be a good referral source for me. I refer with no expectation of guaranteed reciprocity. Of course I want the return referral but I genuinely believe successful networking involves making connections without any expectation-a true *paying it forward*.

This is not how most people approach networking. Have you ever been to a networking event and someone immediately starts rattling off what they do and shoving a business card at you before you even have a chance to say a word? (HINT: don't give your business card until someone asks for it!) Most networkers try to turn the exchange of info into a sales conversation. Sales and networking are not the same marketing activity! I believe successful networking is a lot more about listening than telling. Tell what you do AND listen to what the other person does, but also have a real conversation that gets more to the root of the person—ask about family, group affiliations, where they grew up or where they went to college. It is often through these non-business questions that we get clues of who the person really is and ways that you can connect with them.

I firmly believe that people want to do business with people they know, like and trust. No one gets to know you and like you-and certainly trust you—if all you do is approach them with a litany of your services and a card. In my experience just as a sale takes an average of 5-8 touches either in person, on the phone, through email or social media—I believe a networking relationship also requires that same level of commitment.

While I do make hundreds of connections a year, I do not make those connections lightly. I know the value of my relationships and I do not risk them by cavalierly referring clients and other connections to people I have not vetted by getting more info than a business card and one quick networking conversation. Frankly, networking is a lot like farming—seeds are planted and nurtured as the relationship develops and eventually become a harvest of referrals and connections.

Really successful networking takes time. For me, it is time very well-spent. It is time that has led to finding more great clients, vendors, brand ambassadors and opportunities than I ever could have imagined. I have grown as a person and a business owner from the connections I have made and learned some valuable information about myself and people in general. There is more business opportunity out there than any one of us can handle. From that perspective we really have no competition other than our own limiting beliefs. In business and in networking—just realize I do not have to lose for you to win!

Volunteer Your Way to the Top

Laura B. Baker

Everyone loves a good deal. We all search for a way to get ahead. Are there any short cuts to getting to the top?

Yes! There's an old saying: "It's not *what* you know, but *who* you know." There's a reason why people spend their time volunteering in hospital, schools, and special events all around the world. One, it makes them feel good. Two, it skyrockets them past the masses to the "who you need/want to know" category.

The relationships built while volunteering are priceless, but another benefit is it gives you the opportunity to showcase your skills, dedication and knowledge.

I've spent the better part of the last three decades volunteering for a non-profit educational association. When I began, I was just another face in the crowd. I didn't know anybody and I found it difficult to meet the "right people." My skills and experience were nowhere near the level needed for anyone to give me the time of day, much less anything more than a polite hello and a simple answer to my questions. I quickly found out that I needed access behind Oz' curtain.

Giving your time, energy and available hands opens doors and pulls back curtains. You are always in the right place, at the right time, when you volunteer to help. Even cleaning up after a meeting will open a door to someone or something better than not doing anything. However, the more you volunteer, the more people you meet and more doors will open.

I was quickly able to build relationships with Board Members and Officers of the association I volunteered for all because I was working right by their sides on a continual basis. All those little jobs lead into bigger, more important jobs and a position on the Board of Directors. I was able to learn things and meet people I never would have been able to do had I not offered to help when something needed to be done. And no job or task was too small. Each opportunity to serve lead to another relationship or challenge where I could benefit.

To be honest, the only reason I was able to meet the people I met and do the work I have done was because I was willing to lend a hand and help someone out in the trenches. I don't have the formal education or the employment history to accomplish what I have done without volunteering. I simply didn't have the credentials or the qualifications. All I had was a husband, four (at the time - now 5) kids, and a burning desire to get to know the people and things necessary to improve our lives. It never occurred to me that volunteering would mold and change me in such a dramatic fashion. And it can do the same for you.

Looking for People in All the Right Places

Carol D. Neal

There are many different types of formal networking groups. Obviously, as its CEO, Xperience Connections is one of my favorites, because it fosters great relationships and support for business women. Other well-known groups include eWomenNetwork, Leads, ProNetworker, Business Connect, Business Networking International, Women in Networking, PowerCore, and Power Networking, and COUNTLESS other national and local groups. Check your local newspaper's calendar for Business After Hours listings, lunch mixers, and the like. Also check out your industry's trade associations, such as the American Business Women's Association, Realtor Boards, Credit Professional International, etc. or join your local Chamber of Commerce, alumni group, service association (such as the Elks or Lions Club), and even hobby clubs. All of these are great groups for you to visit to find new referral partners and leads for your own businesses. Costs will vary...some groups have annual or quarterly membership fees in addition to meeting or meal fees...others are free Check out the groups in your area and choose what works best for you...most allow guests to attend free at least once. ASK the people you network with to recommend other groups to you. Evaluate what works for you and what doesn't.

Don't limit yourself to formal networking events. Get involved with a charity, a school, or at your church. Volunteering leads to important connections and the development of relationships that are not based on just building business contacts, but on helping others.

Create your own networking opportunities. Start a book club, garden club, neighborhood watch, or game night. Host a party to honor someone you admire, give an award or even create a scholarship program. There are countless ways of getting people together...all you need is an idea and an invitation. Visit Evite and HouseParty for lots of ideas. Start your own Meetup for a nominal fee and invite your target audience. And don't overlook the value of online groups on Facebook and other networking opportunities on social media, such as LinkedIn, Twitter and Instagram, just to name a few. Most of these are free, and can lead to more face-to-face meetings and networking events. Of course, always exercise caution and common sense when providing information about yourself online or getting together with someone in person that you've met online.

Once you get out there and start meeting people, they will invite you to other events. Don't judge an event in advance; many that seem like they'll be a waste of time often turn out to offer valuable networking opportunities. You never know who's going to be there. And while it's possible you may connect with only one person, that connection could turn into a powerful, long-term relationship that leads you to many other great connections. I made the most impactful connection of my life one day going around the fitness circuit at a Curves for Women when I met the incredible Tracee Randall, who has become my business partner, my coach, my sister, my friend!

Think BIG #1: Build Relationships

Bonnie Ross-Parker

In writing this section to guide you, the reader, to be a more effective networker, the word BIG came to mind. What can I share that would stimulate *your* thinking in a much bigger, broader and more productive way? Then, the idea hit me! Why not use each letter in BIG to emphasize a specific skill that collectively with the other 2 letters could significantly increase results? Hence, the idea behind Think BIG.

Strategy #1: Build Relationships

There are many ideas available to insure that the relationships you have and wish to create can happen. It's important to connect in meaningful and mutually beneficial ways. This is very different from conversations. Conversations are casual; connections are deliberate. Conversations are moments involved in casual exchange; connections are ones that foster ongoing, win-win outcomes. Building on relationships is the cornerstone of all meaningful personal and professional experiences.

One of the best ways to enhance and strengthen connections is by acknowledging appreciation. So often, and I can be just as guilty as the next person, we are grateful to someone for something they said or did and fall short in punctuating our gratitude. We get busy; time passes; we get distracted. None of these 'reasons' are acceptable excuses. There is power in writing and sending a personalized note to the person who has made a difference in your life no matter how big or small. It could be a referral. It could be an invitation to an upcoming event. It could be bringing an article or something relevant and newsworthy to your attention. Whatever it is, it is critical and in fact strengthens relationships to be a person who is conscientious about expressing thanks.

After all, building relationships is about   being and staying connected. Connecting with individuals allows us to become more aware of our behavior, makes us feel good about ourselves and stretches us to achieve our best. You can connect with your team and colleagues to insure each other's success. You can connect with your customers to insure their satisfaction with your products or service and to maintain and increase their business with you.   Sustaining relationships by staying connected is the foundation of your business.

Connecting is not about keeping score. You'll receive payment in ways you might not expect. It all comes down to accessibility. Are you making yourself available? Are you open to helping, suggesting and supporting others and their initiatives? Are you seen as a person who genuinely cares, leads by example and shines the light on the success of others? All of these suggestions are offered to enlighten you and to help you realize that making connections, building relationships and being recognized as one who does are all key elements in giving you the best possible outcome for your time and effort. Once you recognize the value of building relationships, you will truly seek more and more avenues to make to this a top priority.

Think BIG #2: Improve Performance

Bonnie Ross-Parker

Stepping up one's game in a competitive marketplace by being a committed student is clearly the best way to insure business success. It's no longer enough to be average, to get by with basic skills or to think that there isn't someone just waiting to obtain your business! Hence, here are just a few ideas you can implement right now if you are ready and willing to improve your performance. I'm going to focus on three. They are listening skills, personal and professional development and time management.

Strategy #2: Improve Performance

Talking tells and *listening* sells. Period. Successful networkers recognize the value in asking questions, learning from others and initiating conversations. What's the point of doing all the talking when you are NOT the customer? By honing your listening skills, you are actually in the driver's seat, steering the direction of the conversation and positioning yourself to lead where you want the relationship to go. Remember what I said in Build Relationships. Conversations are casual. Connections are deliberate. If you recognize that by listening, you are actually on the lookout for ways to find common ground, for an opportunity to solve a problem for someone, or to be a valued resource, you will significantly separate yourself from anyone else who thinks talking is the way to create business. You and I know better! Listening is an essential ingredient to improve performance.

When it comes to *personal and professional development*, there is simply no excuse for not engaging in the plethora of resources available to learn, to expand one's thinking and to be more effective. Between online and offline classes, webinars, books, other publications, professional newsletters and industry specific networking groups, there exists a wealth of information. You can never learn too much. Commit to implementing the lessons from others who have journeyed before you. Write articles that showcase your expertise. Keep ahead of your competition by identifying who they are. Become familiar with how your products or service differ from what they offer.

In many ways, the difference between being successful and struggling to become a success is largely the difference between being mediocre and being focused on self-improvement. The more you expand your knowledge, the more information you can absorb and apply, the better your outcome. A lot of individuals think knowledge is 'king'. I have to differ. Action is 'king'. While you can capture all the lessons to be learned, listen to all the great masters who inspire, if you don't apply these resources into your performance, ie, *action*, then I can assure you, nothing will happen. The key is simply this. Improve your performance through learning and expect favorable results.

Another way to improve your performance is through *time management*. You can work your business part time or full time. If you are building 'some time', you are engaged in a hobby, NOT in a business! Time management requires planning. You are responsible for your schedule. Plan the tasks necessary to achieve the results you want to achieve. I often get asked, "How much time do you think I should devote to networking?" My answer is always the same: "How much time do you want to schedule to get what you want?" Spend time in the most productive way relative to the time you have. Consider hiring a virtual assistant to do the necessary clerical work that distracts you from business building activity. It's amazing, and you would agree, that everyone is allotted the same amount of time with a 24 hour day. Stop for a moment and think of the incredible accomplishments of individuals you admire. Guess what? They have the same amount of time as you and I. Really? It's all about planning and taking action. It's that simple!

Think BIG #3: Get Bottom Line Results

Bonnie Ross-Parker

If you were asked, "What is the reason you are in business?", the most common answer is: 'to make money'. While popular, that is *NOT* the reason. Want to know what it is? The reason anyone is in business is *to acquire and maintain customers*. One does not 'make money'. It's the customers you have that generate your income. More customers, more income. More satisfied customers, more income. I'm sure you get my point. So, let's close out Think BIG with the final, and perhaps, the most important component of all...results.

Strategy #3: Get Bottom Line Results

The money is in the *follow-up*. What's the point of meeting people, letting them know (eventually) about your products/service and then not following up? Your reputation is effected by the way you do/don't follow-up. Hand-written notes, phone calls and email campaigns are essential if you want to be and stay in front of customers and potential customers. It was a real 'ah ha' for me during a recent training session when the presenter made the following comment: "People buy when *THEY'RE READY* and *NOT* when you want to sell to them." When someone says, 'everyone is a potential customer', that's really a stretch. Someone is only a customer when their need and timing corresponds to what you offer (solution) and when they want their problem solved. How's that for a bit of insight? One of the reasons you want to follow-up and stay on top of your customer or potential customer's mindset, is for the very reason I just stated. You want to be the solution and to be thought of when the need occurs. If you haven't stayed connected, don't expect a favorable outcome. It's that simple.

Let's next address *networking*. While of course I recognize that a lot of 'conversations' are taking place on line, I still think face to face opportunities produce the best results. It's real. It's real time. It's up close and personal. Being an active networker is a great way to build your data base, become known as the go to person for what you offer and build credibility. When I start seeing familiar faces at events, realize they also have a commitment to get out and meet other professionals, I have these individuals on top of my mind when I can generate a potential referral. Again, it's not just about what I can get. It is what can I give that will always come back to me over time? (Remember that speaking engagement I shared that turned into my first and only international keynote?) I'm always on the lookout for new people to meet, to build my data base and for win-win opportunities.

I think of networking as a way to make every connection count. You simply never know where a simple conversation can lead. In The Quick Connection, I mentioned about differentiating yourself, about showing up in a way that others will remember you and about making a difference in the lives you touch. Networking provides the platform. Go into any event with the intention of uncovering treasures. Look for individuals who are already engaged. They are the ones who show confidence. When at the beach, you wouldn't pick up every single sea shell. You'd be attracted to those that are shaped differently, have a certain color arrangement that draws attention or just calls to you. Compare this scenario to networking. Be on the lookout. Hanging out with connections you already have are likely to already be your raving fans. In networking, seek new ones. Implement the strategies shared previously. Amaze yourself!

The last idea I want to share is to be a person that *initiates conversations.*

My motto: *Don't wait. Initiate.* Introduce yourself. Be sure to wear a personalized name tag to make it easier for the other person. Be interested in others. If someone is standing alone, there is no better opportunity to engage in a conversation and put that individual at ease. I call this rescuing. Here's my explanation. When you go up to someone, extend a hand and alleviate their discomfort at standing alone or not knowing anyone, what is the chance that person will be forever grateful? I do this all the time. Believe me, there is nothing more rewarding than building a conversation into a connection when you take the lead! Use open ended questions such as, "Have you been here before? How did you find out about this event? Are there other networking opportunities you attend? What industry do you represent?" (NEVER ask, "What do you do?" That is NOT differentiating yourself because that's what everyone says.) Also, don't lead with work related questions. Your job is to put someone at ease. Offer a compliment. Take the lead to introduce this new individual to someone you know who you spot across the room. Want to build your bottom line? Build on relationships – even casual ones. Rescuing someone is probably one of the best ways to show you care, you're sensitive and generous. People hate feeling self-conscious. They hate walking into an unfamiliar setting with unfamiliar faces. I think it takes a lot of confidence to show up as a newbie. That's the best potential connection of all. You essentially become their hero. Voila!

TIPS ON
SOCIAL MEDIA

"Social media is changing the way we
communicate and the way we are perceived,
both positively and negatively.
Every time you post a photo, or update your status,
you are contributing to your own digital footprint
and personal brand."

~ Amy Jo Martin

The 80/20 of Social Media

Ires D. Alliston

Small business owners today already know that having a presence on social media is not optional. One of the first thoughts that pops into their heads is the immediate need to create a page for their business on every social media network in existence, but the idea of constantly updating and creating content for all of their social media networks can seem daunting. Luckily, Joseph Luran's 80/20 rule of efficiency can be applied to social media marketing whereas 80% is about providing content and value to readers and 20% is self-promotion.

The first step in your social strategy should be to select which networks your business is going to focus on. The same social networks which work for one business won't necessarily work for a different type of business. If you are a B2B engineering business, how many of your customers do you think you'll find on Pinterest? Probably not enough to warrant creating a page where you frequently post. If you sell women's apparel and/or jewelry, on the other hand, Pinterest will be one of your strongest networks. The same principle applies if you own a physical business. Networks like Google+ and Facebook offer a variety of perks for brick and mortar businesses, making them powerful networks to use to meet and connect with customers.

You want to pick the social networks where you'll find the highest density of your target audience. I typically recommend for businesses just starting out with their social media marketing campaign to look at 2 or 3 social networks at first that resonate with their brand (products or services) and set up their accounts on them if they have not already done so. Having 2-3 social networks to start with is manageable compared to having and managing numerous profiles all at once. Next is to post at least 3 times daily on each network, see what works, what doesn't, and evolve your social strategy over time.

Do keep an eye on your Insights and analytics! All social networks now give you handy analytics on how many people you're actually engaging with each post. By making frequent use of their Insights in order to better refine your target audience and what type of content works best, you'll find out what you're doing right and what needs improving. If it's working, keep doing it. On the contrary, if a post gets no audience engagement, find out what you're doing wrong and try that same post on another day next week before you discard it entirely. Peak social media usage times are between the hours of 9 a.m. to 5 p.m. via mobile devices, so by posting something interesting for people to read about, you'll have a better chance of engaging your audience. However, these same peak hours of Facebook activity might not be true for your business if your target audiences are lovers of the nightlife. Essentially, when it comes to posting, try it, test it and tweak it!

Each social network provides its own unique benefits to social media marketing, just as each and every business is unique and has different needs. Keep in mind that there is never one magical social network that will instantly take your marketing strategy (and sales) to the next level, but a combination of using several social networks consistently over a long period of time to first gain the trust of your audience is crucial. An effective way to gain their trust is to provide value consistently plus offer them deals on your products or services as well as tips on your blog. Before you know it, they'll share your content for you.

Lastly, I recommend that business owners create a Google+ page, even if you aren't actually engaging with too many customers. That's because content posted to Google+ historically gets a little boost in the SEO department compared to every other social network.

Attract a Targeted Twitter Following

Angela Hemans

If someone offered you 140 million dollars, would you turn it down? Of course you wouldn't, I don't know too many people who would. Then why do we turn up our noses at the thought that Twitter only has 140 million daily active users compared to the popular Snapchat social network that has 150 million daily users according to Bloomberg[1]?

I consider Twitter to be the *low hanging fruit* of social media. Once you learn how to use the network, then the next step is learning how to attract and connect with a targeted following who will be interested in similar content and offerings you want to share. In this tip, I share 5 ways to help you cut through the ocean of tweets to find potential leads, customers, joint ventures, brand ambassadors, or amplifiers—and more importantly, drive traffic to your website where you have your products and services!

1. Start by following people you are connected with personally on your Facebook profile and who also have an active Twitter account that will be interested in your tweets. You can look for these people by typing their name in the Twitter search box. Remember to try various versions of their name and/or their business name if you don't find them on your first try.

2. Go to the public Twitter lists of people who are in a similar industry. Chances are they will have people on their list that you should get to know too. Twitter lists are usually categorized by interest, profession, geography, or events. Take a few minutes each day to find lists and click through to people's profiles. This tip is particularly my favorite because someone has already

---

[1] http://www.bloomberg.com/news/articles/2016-06-02/snapchat-passes-twitter-in-daily-usage

taken time to compile a list of people who usually turn out to be great future connections.

3. Use tools like *Crowdfire* to help you find your targeted audience. With *Crowdfire*, you can input the @handle of someone in your niche and it will pull up a list of people that follow them. On the free version you can follow up to 25 people per day, so when you do it every day it will add up to about 300 in one week. *Crowdfire* is a great phone app but it can also be used on a desktop.

4. Use event and conference hashtags to connect around a common core interest that can be mutually beneficial for everyone involved. Finding a hashtag that serves a special market being used, in an industry that you serve in will be even more valuable to you and your business. Make a list of all the useful hashtags and over time continue to follow people who are using them.

5. Twitter chats are still one of the most undervalued and underused activities on Twitter. Attend chats in your industry or interests that your target audiences are involved in. Spending 30 minutes in a chat is the easiest way to be part of the conversation and attract followers who are already interested in the same topic. After the chat is over, continue the conversation. You can follow up with that person on Twitter just like you would when attending in-person events.

There are many ways to find and generate leads and there are no wrong or right ways. The key is finding ways that work for you and your business.

The Power of Social Media

Taneka Badie

If you are a business owner trying to sell your products/services, you need to be active on social media. Having the power to connect with a large audience will make users aware of your brand. It is important to make the time to build an online presence. There are several popular social media platforms that you can choose from. You don't need to be on all of them, just choose the ones that work well for your type of business. Once you create a game plan and stay consistent, you will start seeing results over time.

Here are several strategies that should be used to create your game plan:

- Use a calendar to schedule which days you will post on each platform. Also figure which times are best to post according to when users are online the most.
- Use holidays, trending topics, and hashtags in your posts. Facebook, Instagram, and Twitter can be used for these types of posts. If you want your posts to rank high on the Google search engine, incorporate industry specific keywords that people are searching for in your posts.
- Have giveaways to show your customers appreciation. Facebook can be used to share giveaways; boost your posts to get more traffic.
- Ask the users questions to get them to interact. This is also a great way to get feedback. Facebook and Twitter can be used to spark conversations.
- Share content that's related to your industry. This can be used with most social media platforms. Longer content can be used on LinkedIn but keep it under 250 characters on the other social media platforms.

- Share for SumoMe is a tool that is used to share your website on many social media platforms. The more users that share, the more traffic you receive. This tool can increase the amount of shares by 20%. You can try it out for free.
- Create content that is motivational and humorous. Users can get bored easily.
- Create video tutorials related to your products/services. Tutorials can be used on Facebook and YouTube to get your audience to interact and share. Make sure to include these videos on your website and incorporate ways for users to share the videos from your website to social media.
- Share what's happening in your business by posting photos and recording live events. Posts that contains photos and videos are the most engaging. That will give the audience a better connection to your brand. Facebook and Periscope can be used for recording live videos. Instagram can be used for visuals and short 60 second videos. Pinterest is also used for posting visuals.
- Include your social media pages on your website and marketing material.
- Make connections with industry professionals. Find professionals you can build strategic relationships with so you both can grow your businesses. This can be applied by using LinkedIn.
- Know what times to post on each social platform. Here are the best times:

  Facebook between 1:00-4:00 pm
  Twitter between 1:00-3:00 pm
  Instagram between 3:00-5:00 pm
  Pinterest between 8:00-11:00 pm
  LinkedIn between 7:00-9:00 am
  Google+ between 9:00-11:00 am

These strategies will help you take your social media strategy to the next level and see an increase in traffic.

Hypertargeting

Ires D. Alliston

There is a lot that can be said about hypertargeting your customers. Facebook ads, for example, allow advertisers to select from an enormous amount of information when it comes to choosing who will see your ad. The narrower an audience that will see a certain ad, the more effective it will be, and the more money you will save in the long run.

In the same way that Facebook gathers information on all of their users, businesses can incorporate all sorts of useful data in their social media marketing campaigns by gathering information from their fans and followers. This can be a great tool for hypertargeting your consumers who want the products and services that you provide. The best part is that Facebook will do all of the heavy lifting for you when it comes to segmenting your audience and give you an estimate on how many people your ad will reach. There is a wealth of free, public information available that consumers will willingly give you. It's up to your business to take advantage of that information and turn it into a hypertargeted social media marketing campaign.

Each ad campaign you run – regardless of social platform – should have a unique and specific goal. There is a bit of a learning curve when selecting your audience for an ad campaign, but with each ad campaign – even the failed ones – you learn a little more about your audience. A good rule of thumb when running PPC (pay-per-click) ads on social media is to set your daily budget low when you first start out. It won't be long before you create a highly successful ad, and when you do, be sure to save it for future use!

Be Accessible

Ires D. Alliston

One of the main reasons that many companies start a social media marketing campaign is because they want to be more accessible to their customers. If customers have any questions for the company or are hesitant about buying one of their products or services, businesses can always encourage their customers to reach out to them on one of their social networks and ask them anything they want. This has proven to be much more successful than traditional customer service in the last few years, which is a growing trend.

Another reason for companies to create social media marketing campaigns is to increase their visibility to their customers. Today, many people will spend hours on their phones or computers looking at social media. It only makes sense for a business to be where their customers are. Social media marketing is the only form of marketing that can appeal to customers at every stage of the consumer decision journey.

Of the top 10 factors that correlate with a strong Google organic search, seven of those are influenced by social media. If brands are not actively engaged in social media, they will show up less in search engines. Social networks such as Twitter, Facebook and Google+ have a large amount of monthly users; however, the visual media sharing based mobile platforms garner a higher interaction rate when compared to their desktop counterparts. The mobile-only social network, Instagram, for example, has an interaction rate of 1.46% with an average of 130 million users every month, according to Sumangla Rathore and Avinash Panwar, whereas Twitter's interaction rate is a meager 0.3% with 210 million users every month (Capturing, Analyzing, and Managing Word-of-Mouth in the Digital Marketplace, 2016). Does this mean that Instagram is a better marketing platform than Twitter? That all depends on the consumers you are trying to reach.

Tell Your Story in 140 Characters

Angela Hemans

Are you using Twitter to tell your story?

If you're wondering how you can share a story in 140 characters—you can't. But when you string together a bunch of tweets, they can create and develop a powerful storyline that can make an impact on the reader.

I must admit, Twitter wasn't always my favorite social network; I've had a love/hate relationship with it for a number of years. What I learned is that I needed to embrace what made Twitter unique, and accept its uncanny ability to connect and engage people in a full sentence.

Over time, I began to realize that if I strategically develop my tweets into a broken up storyline that they could take my Twitter community on a journey that will make them come back daily to read more of what I had tweeted.

Are you ready to get started building your Twitter story?

First, take a moment to understand the audience with which you're trying to connect. Storytelling is about connecting and finding that relatable point with your community. Not everyone will be able to relate to the story you will tell using your tweets. And that's fine. You only want to attract a certain type of people to your Twitter stream. Who are they? Take a moment and write that down.

Once you know who you are planning to share your Twitter story with, next figure out what story you want to tell. Your story can be about anything, but preferably it will be related to your brand. What is it that you want to share with your community? You are in control; you develop the narrative that will make an impact. If you keep your audience in mind while writing the story, this won't be as difficult as it may seem.

If you're still wondering what kinds of stories to tell here are a few tips to get you on your way:

- Create a story of tweets on a topic that is of interest to your audience.
- Discuss a previous trending topic, share your thoughts, and ask questions that will get your audience involved.
- Share an emotional story, that makes you relatable to your audience on a deeper level, and don't forget to use pictures.
- Do you have an event coming up? Create buzz by tweeting about the journey you're on and all the ups and downs that are happening.

Your story can be about anything, as long it is what your audience will find interesting, valuable, or entertaining.

Lastly, although your tweets are 140 characters, make sure to create cohesiveness among each story. You can do this by making sure your tweets all have a similar tone. So you don't want to be sarcastic in one tweet but completely serious or funny in the next. The tone in tweets can be easily misunderstood, and taken out of context even with a smiley face emoji. Keep things simple. When you're creating the tweets, write them together, make them each 140 characters and then read it to make sure it's all cohesive.

Storytelling in 140 characters may seem difficult, but once you've created a few and shared them, it becomes easier to do. Over time you will find an audience that will connect with you on an authentic level and that's when the possibilities begin to open up.

Can They Find You?

Carol D. Neal

One of my pet peeves is what I call "broken links" on Facebook.

Now, I realize that some people like to keep their "personal" Facebook page separate from their business life, so as not to overwhelm friends and family with their business doings, and that's OK. Those people obviously would not want to have links to their business website on their personal page. But to increase their odds for success in their business endeavors they could create a separate business page, and the tip I'm giving here applies to that page just as it would to someone who shares their business on their personal page.

Wherever you list your business, make sure the resulting link actually goes to YOUR business page or website. Here are some common mistakes to avoid:

1. Being too vague. Too often we see someone list simply that they are "self-employed" or a "coach", and the link takes people to the sad little "blue briefcase" waiting rooms on Facebook.

2. Sending the link to the company website instead of your own if you are in Direct Sales.

3. Having a typo in your URL that results in the link going nowhere.

It only takes a few seconds to double-check your links by clicking on them yourself after they are posted, and those few seconds could save you embarrassment as well as lost income. As an event organizer and networking leader, I get very frustrated if it isn't easy for me to figure out what industry a person is in and locate the right links to their website or Facebook page if I'm trying to promote them on social media.

Imagine how much more quickly a potential customer who does not know you will give up!

In addition to making sure your links are correct on your Facebook page, make sure they are correct anytime you post them on Facebook or Twitter. If you add your websites or Facebook pages to daily posting ladders, you always want to go back after you hit "post" and make sure the link works there as well, and that your preview displays properly. If there's an error, delete and resubmit, or edit the original post. Please don't just keep adding more comments until you get it right, especially if you start the correction with the word "Oops!" You are drawing attention to yourself then for the wrong reason.

Not only do you want people to be able to find the proper page or website so they can actually connect and do business with you, remember that you are creating an impression of YOU, and impressions do matter!

Find Your Customer Voice

Ires D. Alliston

One of the little known perks of establishing a strong social media network for your business is access to a wealth of marketing information and your customer voice. Things which might often be overlooked by companies are the comments section on blogs, content communities, and in forums. These consumer comments may provide a valuable feedback on your products, or products similar to yours that are currently used by your same target audience.

A smart business will listen to their customers' voice, hear the feedback that they are leaving, and work on adapting to their complaints, compliments, and needs. Even if the customer voice is not directly related to your company, your products or service, if it is something that comes from a member of your target audience, you can rest assured that it is valuable input which should be considered by your business.

Facebook, Twitter and Instagram, as well as third party social media apps such as Hootsuite, all provide access to detailed information regarding who your most loyal fans and followers are. These insights are one of the most powerful tools in your social media toolbox for nurturing leads and increasing conversions.

Of course, managing your social media channels goes far beyond simply analyzing data. If your audience is engaging you, be sure to engage them back in some playful conversation! Your response to customer service inquiries doesn't always have to be serious and professional. For instance, if your audience is in their 20s, feel free to throw a couple of jokes into your response. This is all a part of building rapport.

You should also be actively inviting your followers to bring up any comments, critiques, or feedback they have on your products or services to send you a message on social media.

Likewise, when you do not engage your audience's comments or do not respond to questions, it can be harmful to your brand in general. When people feel like they've been done a disservice, they like to tell their friends about it, and whose side do you think their friends are going to take?

Automate Your Twitter Feed

Angela Hemans

Automation seems like a dirty word in business; this is a hot discussion topic for many small business owners and entrepreneurs. Automation tools are either recommended or not considered a business necessity. Twitter automation tools are needed so that you can keep a consistent presence online, and so that you can spend your time doing money-making activities for your business. Let's face it, to run a successful business, you can't spend all day and night following people, tweeting, retweeting, and engaging in conversations unless that is part of your business model. And for most of us that is not the case. When you use the right tools, it's like having a personal VA for your Twitter account. There are quite a few helpful desktop tools and apps that I use in my every day routine that I highly recommend.

Social Oomph

This desktop program has a freemium version and a pro version. I started out using the free but then eventually upgraded to the pro version for some of its upgraded features. With the free version you can create reusable Twitter updates and with the paid version, you can create content queues to hold all of your evergreen tweets you will want to share over time on a rotation. You can schedule tweets around the clock or with a few clicks schedule them for certain days and times. The downside of this tool is at first it can seem clunky, but once you get used to it, you will spend only a few minutes updating and scheduling. You can use *Social Oomph* to find Twitter followers and create private DM messages. (Side note: I don't recommend sending DM tweets in the beginning when you're growing your account, save that for a later time.) And this tool does not have a mobile app, but otherwise is a great program to consider.

TweetDeck

Tweetdeck is only a desktop tool, now owned by Twitter, and it has a great user interface. It has many features to offer, go to the website and check them out. I'll be sharing just a few of the features here. Like *Social Oomph*, you can schedule tweets, but it doesn't have a way to store your evergreen content. If you have a virtual assistant or someone that handles your Twitter account, the great thing about *Tweetdeck* is that you can provide them access on the platform without actually giving them your Twitter password. Did I mention that *Tweetdeck* is a completely free tool to use? There is no paid option as of 2016.

CrowdFire App

Need to schedule tweets on the go? Then the *Crowdfire* app is good tool for when you have an idea you want to tweet later. It has a simple interface that you can use, with other features such as finding Twitter followers, unfollowing, and finding lookalike audiences of your competitors. This app has a freemium and two low-cost upgrade options and can be downloaded by both IPhone and Android users. If you're looking for a well-rounded app that can schedule content, help you grow and engage with your Twitter community then *Crowdfire* is a great pick.

Even though I'm mainly talking about Twitter tools for automation, *Social Oomph* can be used for other social networks like Facebook groups and pages, as well as for LinkedIn profiles. *TweetDeck* is only for Twitter. And *Crowdfire* app is for Twitter and Instagram. Automation serves a purpose, and when it's used effectively it frees up your most precious commodity—TIME! Time that you can now use to grow an interactive and impactful online community.

Say It With Video

Laura B. Baker

Do you want to generate more interest for your business?

Videos are taking over social media and it is no longer an "up-and-coming" marketing strategy. It's here and it isn't going away anytime soon. It's a powerful way to communicate with an audience. Live video gives the small (and big) company's business owner an instant and credible way to build their brand, explain their value, and immediately build relationships with customers and prospects.

According to Brightcove, videos generate 1200% more shares than text and images combined. Both Instagram and Facebook are currently pushing video content to the forefront because that is what people want to see, and it is a great way to humanize your business.

Statistics show it is working quite well. By easily including a video on a landing page it can increase conversion rates by 80%. 92% of mobile video customers share videos with other people. It is also important for the videos to look good both with sound and without sound. People are watching at work.

While comedy and music videos are the most popular, news videos command a respectable third place.

Michelle of World Wide Launch says: "Of all the content type I post, video gives me the best return. Videos allow my brands the ability to communicate who they are effortlessly."

YouTube reports that mobile video consumption is rising 100% every year, while video ads increase purchase intent by 97% and brand association by 139%.

Dropping a video in an email leads to 200-300% increase in click-through rates.

These numbers are serious. Just as the introduction of TV changed households from sitting next to the radio back in the 1940's and 1950's, video is revolutionizing social media. Sesame Street has changed our brains. We can no longer sit and wait for information to be rolled out for us. We crave instant gratification. Video fills our compulsion to get our information immediately, and smart business owners are jumping on board to collect the revenue that is being generated.

Twitter Networking: Cultivate New Connections

Angela Hemans

"If a man does not make new acquaintances as he advances through life, he will soon find himself alone."   ~ Samuel Johnson

Can you make a valuable connection using Twitter? Yes, you can, and I am my own case study. It's because of the relationships I've built through networking on Twitter that I am able to write these tips for you in this book that I know you will find helpful.

Networking on Twitter can be a bit daunting at times, but it is no different than networking in real life. I have a few simple Twitter networking etiquettes that will help you cultivate new connections that can turn into potential sales leads, referral partners, or a good friend and mentor.

Create Brand Consistency
Twitter is just one part of your digital footprint. Facebook, Snapchat, Instagram, Linkedin--in this digital age chances are you are on at least two networks and most people are likely on more. Having a consistent brand image across networks is important when you're networking online. Once someone finds you on Twitter and takes an interest in you, chances are they will want to connect with you elsewhere. Having different identities on different platforms is a turn off which will cause others to be confused and standoffish when it comes to doing business with you. Your Twitter bio and content can be slightly different on each platform, but having social identities under one name should be the main priority, while creating content that is consistent with each network's culture.

Know Your Reason for Networking on Twitter
Understanding what kind of relationships you would like to develop on Twitter will determine your overall Twitter strategy to implement. If you want to create a robust referral community for your business, the

types of people you want to connect with will most likely be different from people you may want to have as an accountability partner. What these two groups find interesting and valuable to them will be different. How you plan on connecting and engaging with them will also be different. Building a network of the "right people" is key to successful networking using Twitter.

Listen To Attract Your Network

Before you begin tweeting content to attract your ideal audience to you, listen first and see what conversations are taking place with your potential network. What types of content are they sharing, retweeting, and commenting on Twitter? Once you know what they find valuable, now you have a mutual point of interest, which leads to the next point.

Be Engaging

Not sure what to say when you're engaging on Twitter? Are you overwhelmed by the thought of it? Try a few of these openers and remember it's just 140 characters.

- Find an original tweet or article by the person of interest and share your thoughts about it in a quoted retweet.
- Like a few tweets you find interesting from that person, not only will it show your interest in the value they provide but it will put you on their radar of engaging people. It's like giving someone a compliment—and who doesn't like a compliment?
- If they retweeted or liked any of your tweets, thank them in a private Twitter message (a direct message) and keep the conversation going.

Don't over complicate the process. You wouldn't interrupt someone at a networking event and just start talking about yourself. The same rules apply for networking on Twitter. Connecting on this network is about cultivating a *relationship-first* mentality. Use your tweets to continue the conversations and consistently engage. And when the time is right, seek out opportunities to follow up off the Twitter network, either by phone, Skype, or even in-person if they are local.

Engage

Ires D. Alliston

If you can only do one thing during your social media marketing campaign, make sure that you are engaging your audience with interesting content. It's also easy to monitor the content you create by monitoring the number of views you get.

Now it's one thing to simply post content on your company's social network regarding the recent deals available on your products or services, but it's entirely different to post quality content that will engage and entertain your audience. This is the type of content that gets shared by social networks users and makes its way around the internet until it goes viral.

Through the use of quality, engaging content, each consumer takes the responsibility of the marketing department by sharing your content with their friends, family and social network. This is a fundamental part of social media marketing.

But engagement is a two-way street. Companies should not only be posting their own engaging content, but also sharing the content of others that they find interesting. The content you share with your social network friends and followers doesn't necessarily have to be related to your products or service. The point of sharing and reposting other people's engaging content is to bond with them and keep them engaged. They will appreciate a short, funny video popping up in their social network streams from time to time and thank you for sharing it with them.

On that note, it is also important for companies to engage their consumers by responding to their comments. Regardless of what their comment is about or what they commented on, a company is able to humanize themselves by actively engaging other people in the comments field.

This has distinct advantages over traditional marketing and advertising, which is limited to a one-way interaction. You have something that you want to show or tell your audience and you make sure that they see it, but there isn't any feedback. They can't tell you what they like or dislike about it. Consumers do not like the stigma of having to call customer service, no matter how great a customer service you may have. Social media is the only true way to actively engage your customers in casual conversation, to connect with them, and to receive their casual feedback on your products or services.

Using Hashtags Successfully on Twitter

Angela Hemans

Hashtags have become an invaluable tool for researching certain topics or branding an event, and they are a cost-effective way to track content or build your business brand. A simple way to think of a hashtag is that they are keywords with a # symbol attached to them. So if you've already done your keyword research, then you have done most of the work when it comes to hashtags.

I can't tell you how many times that I personally have used them to connect with people in specific niches that I'm interested in. It's now part of my own marketing hack, which I include in some of my online marketing strategies that I use for myself and with my clients. If you're not quite sure about using hashtags, I'll share how it can fit into your social business activities on Twitter.

Why you should be using Hashtags for brand awareness:

If you're doing any type of online business, then hashtags will most likely be incorporated into your social media plan at some point in time. Use them to expand the reach of your audience and increase the engagement of the content you have created. You can use hashtags to demonstrate your knowledge in your niche and be the *go to* source for information.

Hashtags can be beneficial for keeping track of content that your audience has an interest in and enjoys sharing over the internet. It's a great tool you can use to keep you connected to the various topics being discussed. Communities all over Twitter are having Twitter chats, and to keep up with the conversation, specific hashtags are being used as a way to keep all the tweets together. Hashtags are just another channel to spread your message, so why not start making hashtags a part of your strategy?

If you are unsure where to start, a great first step is to consider using a branded hashtag. This tactic is created for the purpose of recognizing which of your branded content is the most relevant to your audience. Creating a branded hashtag doesn't have to complicated. Start with the name of your company if it's not too long. Or you can use a phrase that is part of your business message that you frequently use. Keep it simple and memorable! One thing to remember when you're creating a branded hashtag, make sure it's not attached to any suspicious or undesirable conversation, i.e. sexually explicit content. Use a tool like *hashtagify.me* or do a simple Google search for the hashtag you want to use and see what comes back. A little research now can save you and your business from a whole lot of future headaches and hassles.

Hashtags are weighed differently within each social media platform. When you consider any of the 5 major social networks, Facebook, Twitter, Google plus, LinkedIn, and Instagram, hashtags are still a valuable and underused feature by the communities on these platforms. Twitter is technically the birthplace of hashtags. They are incredibly important for increasing the engagement and branding awareness.

Here's an advance search pro tip for expanding your business message. On Twitter, type the (#) plus your keywords to help you find your target audience and use those same keywords to drive traffic to your content by cross promoting it on different social platforms like Facebook using the same hashtag. Find trending hashtags that you can use by going to sites like hashtag.org, Trendsmap.com, or Ritetag.com. As you're compiling all of these hashtags, remember many of them you will want to re-use on a continuous basis. Keep track of them by making a list of them and your reason for using them, so you can have it as a point of reference when creating Twitter content.

Be mindful of hashtag etiquette; as with anything in life, too much of anything becomes a problem and that is the same for using hashtags in social media; but hashtags are a great connector and useful feature every small business owner should include in their social media plan.

TIPS ON
DIRECT SALES

"If you are working on something exciting that you
really care about, you don't have to be pushed.
The vision pulls you."

~ Steve Jobs

Your List is Your Business Plan

Carole Cheatam

Everyone knows that every successful business begins with a business plan. I've always disliked preparing a business plan for the traditional businesses I owned and my network marketing business was no exception. Day two of my training, I was tasked to make a list of everyone I knew. I thought, that's not necessary; I have most of my contacts in my email address list and my Blackberry. No need to write down what already existed. Because my business started out on such a positive note....I had several friends and family who joined with me as promoters and customers, and I was helping them duplicate what I had done. Feeling pretty confident that we were well on our way to being successful earners, I never even trained them in the need to make a list. But soon business started to slack off, and we had pretty much contacted our immediate family and friends, referred to in the industry as a "warm market."

Because our Atlanta market was growing so rapidly, I had the good fortune of meeting with and being mentored by one of our co-founders and a multi-millionaire earner in the industry. I loved those meetings, he would share so many valuable nuggets, and he was so encouraging. Although, I was 20+ years his senior, I would tease him that he was one day older than me because his birthday was one day before mine. One night at dinner, the dreaded list was the subject of conversation. I tried to blend into the scenery and hoped he would forget I was present. Of course, I was not so lucky; and I had to admit that I hadn't even started my list. He explained to me that my list was my business plan, and if I planned to succeed, I needed to complete a list of everyone I knew. "Everyone," I asked....."Everyone," he said! That night I couldn't wait to get home, and I made a list of 200 people; I felt so accomplished. Now that it was completed, I put it in a very nice labeled folder and placed it in a file. Several weeks later when our co-founder was visiting again, he made it a point to ask if I'd completed the list and how many were on the list. I was excited to tell him I had in fact completed it and I had a walloping 200 people on it. He leaned his head to the side and laughingly said, "Didn't you say you were 65 years old, and you only know 200 people; where have you been?" "You mean everybody"? I queried. Once again, he patiently said "Everybody"!

I balked that I didn't know all of their numbers anymore, that I hadn't been in touch with some of them in years, and some I only knew by first name. I can still remember him saying to me that I needed to get the names out of my head and onto paper; take them out of my phone and onto paper; take them off the computer and onto paper; and he promised that it would make a huge difference. He was so right!! First of all, I ended up with over 600 people on my list. No, I didn't have numbers for some, but what was so surprising is I would sometimes encounter someone who knew the same person and was able to get their updated information. I can't tell you how many people I was able to find on Linked In and Facebook. I haven't even been able to get through the entire list yet and it's been almost 6 years since I completed it. But I've reconnected with some amazing people, and been instrumental in coaching them as they pursue their health and fitness goals. And yes, as I begin the training with my new team members, I emphasize the importance of their business plan.

Goals Are Key

Susan Guthrie

Definition of a Goal: An observable and measurable end result having one or more objectives to be achieved within a more or less fixed time-frame.

When setting your goals for life and business set them high! Set your goals with the finish line in mind.

Napoleon Hill's six steps to success when setting goals are:
1) Be definite as to the amount that you want to have or achieve.
2) Determine exactly what you intend to give in return.
3) Establish a definite date when you intend to possess what you desire.
4) Create a clear plan for carrying out your desire and begin at once, whether you are ready or not, to put this plan into action.
5) Write out a clear, concise statement of what you intend to acquire, name the time limit for its acquisition, state what you intend to give in return for it, and describe clearly the plan through which you intend to accumulate it.
6) Read your written statement aloud twice daily, once just before retiring at night and once after rising in the morning. AS YOU READ, SEE AND FEEL AND BELIEVE YOURSELF ALREADY IN POSSESSION OF THE GOAL.

Write a vision statement. Reading your vision statement aloud twice daily as an affirmation is the most important step. After you write your plan, verbalize your intentions, visualize it happening and keep it in front of you in pictures.

Create a vision board with your goals for the year. Cut out photos of the items you desire and post them where you will see them daily. Be specific as to what you really want. Be careful to only include items that you truly desire on your board.

You need a clear plan of attack with daily, weekly, monthly and yearly goals. You need to know where you are at reaching your goals at all times. Course-correct as you need to.

Remember the saying, "Out of sight, out of mind." Keep your goals and dreams in front of you at all times.

Denis Waitley said, "The reason that most people don't reach their goals is that they don't define them, learn about them, or seriously consider them as believable and achievable."

The size of your goal will determine how much time that you spend on your business. If you have a large goal, then plan to spend a lot of time on your business. Know your numbers. If you want to earn a six-figure income over $100,000, you'll need to earn $8,300 per month and about $270 per day. How many customers, business builders, and team leaders do you need to hit those goals?

Eric Worre says the truth is enough. The Network Marketing opportunity is amazing. Remember the 1-3-5-7 formula when setting your goals in Network Marketing. It will take one year to become competent and start making some money in your business. It will take three years to replace your current full-time income. It will take five years to make six figures and seven years to become world class. Anything worthwhile takes time.

Remember, it is not "Net-wish Marketing, it is Network Marketing." It is not necessarily "What you think about you bring about." It is more likely "What you think about most, plan and work for, you bring about."

Set your goals high, develop your plan, visualize your results and don't give up until you achieve them.

Wax the Car!

Tracee Randall

In 2007 I had never been a part of the direct sales industry, and I was as "green as green can be." In hindsight I am quite sure that my upline was labeling me as "ignorance on fire"--I was definitely building a huge team quickly and moving up in the ranks without any idea how!

That upline turned out to be my first mentor. I learned so much from him. Not just about how to build my business, but how to live my life and grow myself. I will never forget this statement he said to me, "You are the same today as you will be 5 years from now, except for the books you read and the people you meet." He was quoting another great man, Charles "T" Jones, but I didn't know that at the time!

Mentors. Another great quote I heard was this, "There are two ways to learn--you can either learn from mistakes or mentors". Well, I had certainly made a whole lot of mistakes up to that point, and it made sense to learn from those who had gone before me.

It takes being humble to learn from a mentor, and pride is one of the enemies of success. A friend will love you no matter what; a mentor will love you enough to help you change.

I love the movie "Karate Kid"-- the first one, where Mr. Miagi teaches Daniel how to wax his car. He took Daniel's hand and made the motion to the left and to the right--I can hear his voice "Wax on. Wax off." Daniel is so impatient. He insists that this is a waste of time, he has come to Mr. Miagi to teach him how to fight, and he certainly doesn't see what waxing MR. MIAGI'S CAR has to do with karate! But Daniel is obedient even if he doesn't understand the training. Day after day they train--Mr. Miagi sitting on his front porch drinking lemonade, Daniel sweating in the hot sun waxing the car. The test is passed when Daniel is jumped from behind and without thinking he took his assailants to the ground in one swift motion. It was the strength in his hands and wrists from the unrelenting hours of repetitive motion AND the subconscious reaction that won the battle. Sometimes, no, *much* of the time, a mentor will assign you a task that you do not understand and it is in the obedience of following it without question that sets you apart from the rest. Another way to say it is that you are "teachable and coachable."

Over the past few years, as my conventional and my direct sales businesses grew, I have often had people ask me if I will mentor them. It is definitely a compliment to be asked, but most of the time people don't understand the role of the mentor and that of the mentored. The person being mentored must *earn* the time and energy of the mentor. Most people see someone being successful and they want to follow them around, shadow them and think that is enough. But it's not. It takes time and trust to establish the relationship. It takes nurturing and it takes dedication on the part of the one requesting to be mentored. In order to earn the attention of a mentor you must do what others will not do. You must be willing to go where they go, stay up late and get up early—you must be willing to "serve" and even honor them.

I love the story of the young Tony Robbins who at 17-years-old walked into the office of the successful Jim Britt requesting to be coached and mentored. Jim laughed him off saying "come back when you're 18, kid." I can't remember the exact details, but it was Tony's persistence and consistency that won Jim over, and finally Jim agreed to mentor Tony—and well, the rest is history!

How do you gain the attention and the direction of a mentor? Someone who is qualified to mentor you has earned that position through hours of dedication himself, years of practicing the craft, staying up late while others slept, getting up early, going places where others would not go. With their position comes lots of sacrifice, so it is important that you respect that position, and you must EARN his attention as well. If you trust your mentor, then you must be willing to follow his direction without question, and to do the "little things" that don't seem to matter—you must be willing to stand in the hot sun and wax the car!

No, No, No, No, No!

Carole Cheatam

I remember how excited I was to begin my new venture in the direct sales industry. The company I chose had very successful results, and I, too, was experiencing a great transformation. I couldn't wait to tell everyone I knew how great our products were and how they needed to join me to become financially successful as I intended to be. Fortunately, the first few people I spoke with saw the value and came on board too!! But then I got my first "no." Wait, did I just hear that right? We've been friends for years, and you don't want to join me or purchase any of these great products? And then there was the second "no." Wow, you've got to be kidding, we're related. Do you know how many days it took me to get over the first "no"...how could you be saying "no" too?

Too quickly, there were more "no's" than "yes's". I find it humorous when I think of it now; but, I was devastated then. Like so many others when they first become a part of this industry, I associated the "no" as a personal rejection. I went to a meeting where the speaker shared how he felt rejected too when he heard his first "no." Like me, he wanted to go home and lock himself in for at least a month, and the second and third "no's" didn't make it any easier. But one day he decided he'd change his strategy. Rather than meet people and expecting a "yes," he'd set the expectation of receiving a "no;" his goal that day was to get five "no's." As easy as that sounded, I assure you it wasn't. But I decided, if I were going to succeed in this business, I'd need to be able to handle the successes as well as the rejection. But then something unexpectedly happened. I received a call from someone who previously had no interest requesting a meeting and more information. That person became a business partner of mine; and, when I asked why she changed her mind, she said she didn't. When she originally said no, it was because she had other commitments and felt it wasn't the right time. For me, that was a HUGE lesson learned...."no" doesn't necessarily mean not ever, it can mean not now.

But the real learning experience came about when I was at lunch one afternoon. One of my acquaintances that I had approached was happy to tell me that she was now taking our products and had already had great success. I was a little confused, because I knew she had not placed an order with me. As it turns out, someone else had approached her as well, and at a time when she was ready to start her fitness goal. She said since she hadn't heard from me again, she just decided to order from someone else. Boy did that sting! What did I learn from this? The fortune is in the follow-up...48% of people never follow-up and 80% of sales are made on the 5th to 12th contact.

So, if you're reading this and you ever said "no," you can expect a call from me!

Personal Philosophy

Susan Guthrie

Definition of Philosophy: The study of ideas about knowledge, truth, the nature and *meaning* of life, etc.

Your personal philosophy has been formed by what you have learned or experienced so far in your life. I attribute most of my personal philosophy to my Dad, Robert Glenn Weaver. He taught me to work hard, give back to others, and live a life of integrity.

Over the years, you have been influenced by the words people say, songs, books, television, movies, and events both good and bad. Each piece of information creates a new belief, and how you use this information is up to you. You can choose to allow negative conversations or events block the achievements of your goals. Don't allow negativity to sabotage your dreams. Choose where you spend your time wisely.

Review and revise your personal philosophy to represent your belief in yourself. Look at your past mistakes and learn from them. Find a mentor who is successful in your field and model their behavior. Become a good listener. Be selective in who and what you listen to. If the message is ignorant or negative tune it out. Don't spend a lot of time listening to talk radio, news stations, negative people or other "trash". Learn to listen for information or a message that resonates with you and your goals.

Jim Rohn once said, "The art of listening is an opportunity to add to our knowledge and to increase our value. The process of speaking, on the other hand is the act of putting on display all—or the little—that we have learned. We must first master the art of listening before our spoken words will have any great value to others."

You have two ears and one mouth—use them in that ratio.

Read! Most people don't read at all. The easiest way to educate yourself it to read good books. Commit to reading at least 10 pages of personal development per day. Read books to inspire you to do and be better.

Keep a gratitude journal. Keeping a journal is a great way to see how your life has changed and improved. Writing down all of the people and things that you have learned from and you are grateful for will remind you how blessed you are.

The formula for success: Daily discipline will move you toward your goals or away from them, and your level of self-discipline will have a direct impact on your success. Read books that pertain to your business or personal development. Journal, attend classes, listen and observe more. In order to change your outcome you must change your thinking. How we do anything is how we do everything. You have the choice to be disciplined or disappointed.

The main reason that most people are not successful in life and business is neglect. It is easy to get out of the habit of the daily disciplines of reading, exercise, etc. that make you a better person. Neglecting the little things will turn into big things—small choices can greatly impact your confidence.

It's important for all of us to review and revise our personal philosophies daily to stay on track and to be who we are destined to be.

Don't Quit Your Day Job (Too Soon)

Dannella Burnett

The Direct Sales Industry or MLM Companies can be an awesome way to create wealth, generate multiple streams of income or simply earn a few hundred extra dollars per month and enjoy a quality product line at a wholesale price as a distributor. There are many mistakes that people can make though in starting up a DS company and many ways to improve your mindset and activities to have greater success.

One mistake that I've seen many make is seeking a DS company with the immediate goal of replacing their current job. I do think that replacing a job you dislike or that limits your freedom of time or expression is a good goal to have but I've seen many make that leap too soon.

When you first start with a Direct Sales company you usually have two objectives – build a base of retail customers and build a team of like-minded individuals to also build a base of retail customers. Both are important in most DS companies in order to have success and generate income. While a goal might be to quit the day job, I've seen many get their initial success by sharing their new products with their coworkers and new people they may meet through that job. Quitting the day job too early can actually hurt your progress towards your ultimate goals by reducing the number of people that you can expose to your product, service or opportunity!

Success Is a Mind Game

Jody P. Humphrey

Mindset is important in all aspects of life, but never more so than in building a super successful multi-level marketing team. You must have confidence—confidence in your product, confidence in the system, confidence in the concept, confidence in the compensation system, but most importantly confidence in YOU. Personal development is the most important investment you can make toward the success of your career in direct sales. Always be a student—continually learn and grow your skills.

This is true not only for yourself but as a leader of a team. You must become a Director of Motivation. Ultimately motivation has to come from within—but your success in direct sales and in building a large team hinges on your ability to motivate your team—not just through words but through actions. You must be the hardest worker in your business. Your team will watch what you do more than what they hear. Motivating your team also includes giving them the tools they need. Making sure they know about the next event, call, training or presentation. You can't make them go but make sure they know!

Part of motivating is making sure you and your team focus on the front end of your business. Master the basics so you can do them over and over. You have to focus on the right things. What is your belief level, your willingness to work, and your commitment level? Focusing on this for yourself and helping your team members focus on this will multiply results for both you and your team. But remember belief in yourself, the product and the system is the foundation for success. But belief comes from action. Action does not come from belief. Make a plan and work the plan.

Begin with the end in mind—have a leadership mindset—both as a leader of your own thoughts and actions and for leading your team. Harness the power of your beliefs.

March to the Beat of Your Own Drummer

JoBeth Martin

I think it is tempting as we walk the path of entrepreneurship to look at what someone else is accomplishing and want to duplicate what they are doing to get the success they are having. Naturally, we can learn a great deal from someone else's success and failures. We would be wise to see what has worked for others and tweak it to make it our own for our business. The drive and success of others can be a huge motivation for us to envision something bigger, step out in faith and take the risk that we may have been unwilling to take. When you see people that you really admire as business leaders and successful individuals who have accomplished great things, stop and ask yourself a few questions.

What is it about that person that I admire? What is the price they have paid for their success? Am I also willing to pay the same price? Does the way that they have done business fit into my belief system and my priorities in life? What can I learn from them that will impact my journey? What is specific to their journey that really doesn't fit for me?

As you answer these questions it will help you focus on what is important to you and where you need to grow. You may discover an area that you need to just go for it! You need to take that risk and step out in faith. Sure it is scary but the honest truth is that to grow as an entrepreneur you have to be willing to do the new and scary things and take the risk.

Know yourself and know what you believe about life and what success means to you. Ask the hard questions and be honest with your answers. Be okay with the answer that is right for you. Perhaps the best place to start is with your belief system and what is a non-negotiable priority for you in life. If you can come to business as a whole person you will have so much more value to add. What you learn as you pay attention to your own journey will make you a more impactful and intriguing person to others.

Here is the balance; understand your beliefs, priorities and life circumstances and how they fit into the pace that you can grow your business. But don't allow your life circumstances and potential limiting beliefs to hold you back. How does that play out in real time with your business? For me personally a huge priority is to continue to impact my grown children in a positive way. I have a husband, five daughters, three sons-in-law, and 4 grandchildren. If an overriding priority is to impact their lives I will choose to make time for them. Of course there are times when I could be involved in a business activity but choose to give time to family. This is an intentional choice that I make. Does it mean I occasionally miss an event that may positively impact my business? Of course! Is it worth it? Absolutely it is worth it because that decision is consistent with my overall journey and that end goal that I have in mind. Conversely, could I use them as an excuse to slack off and not stretch to grow my business? Yes, again. But that also would not accomplish the goals of my journey.

In order to accomplish the calling I have to be crystal clear about my priorities and I make choices accordingly. I choose to RESPECT MY JOURNEY AND MARCH TO THE BEAT OF MY OWN DRUMMER!

Set Goals, Dream Big, and Please Pass the Tissues

Carole Cheatam

According to the Direct Sales Association, in 2015 over 20 million people were involved in direct selling; about 77% of those were women, and in the US alone sales totaled over $35 billion. Direct Sales has become one of the most successful methods of providing products and services to the consumer, with most of the sales being generated by health and wellness companies.

With those stats who wouldn't be wowed and wooed! I had owned traditional businesses before, but with those came employees, overhead, inventory, and too many other headaches. I got really excited with the fact that for a mere fraction of what it would normally cost for a start-up I could have a business where I could work from home, work when I wanted, meet hundreds of people, and have income potential based on how hard I worked....or not!

The company I joined was like most in that they offered mentorship and training. The two areas that were heavily emphasized were setting goals and dreaming big. Now goal setting was absolutely not foreign to me, it's something I had done most of my adult life, but I realized the goals I had previously set were all long term goals. My goals now were broken down as lifetime, long term and short term, along with desired dates of achievement.

Dreaming big was a little bit more challenging; I'm more of a pragmatist and never really spent a lot of time dreaming. And certainly none of my former employers had ever encouraged me to dream. In fact when I really thought about it, they were the ones with the big dreams and I was helping to fulfill them. I was tasked to create a "lived" list, similar to a bucket list but without the connotation to dying. With this exercise I was to deeply reflect on what my life would be like if money were no object, if I could live anywhere I wanted, if I could spend my time with anyone I wanted, and if I could have anything I wanted.

Sharing my list with my mentor, he pointed out that my list wasn't filled with cars, homes, jewelry and material things but filled with experiences; my dreams were for my children and grandchildren and generations to come. My dream was to change the financial landscape of my family. In the industry there's a quote that I had heard but never really thought much about and that was "Your 'why' will make you cry." He helped me identify that my "WHY" was my family! He explained that my "why" would keep me enthusiastic; my "why" would motivate me to keep pushing forward when I really felt like quitting; my "why" would keep me running towards the goals I had set.

As I sat and listened I realized that I had made the right decision to become a part of an industry that would afford me the opportunity to put the wheels in motion to fulfill my dreams, and I quietly said, "Please pass me the tissues."

MOMENTUM – The Need for Speed

Susan Guthrie

Definition of Momentum: The strength or force that something has when it is moving; the strength or force that allows something to continue or to grow stronger or faster as time passes.

The key to growth in your Network Marketing business is Momentum. When you first begin your business there is a natural hesitancy to get started. You might be still learning about the products, organizing the brochures, etc. These are important, but don't spend too much time on trying to get perfect before you start. The longer you delay in launching your business the harder it will be to get it off the ground. Don't suffer from "Analysis Paralysis."

Walt Disney once said, "The best way to get started is to quit talking and begin doing."

Steps to launch your business:

Make the decision that this is what you really want to do. You must be committed because the first few people to say no will knock you out of the game before you get started. Typically, it is your family or close friends who will say no first. Don't take it personally, just put them on your 'maybe later' list.

Find a mentor in your business who is very successful, typically someone who is financially linked to you. Ask if you can shadow them to learn exactly what they do to become successful. Then do just that! Most people who are new to Network Marketing find ways that they can "improve" things – don't go down that rabbit hole. The current systems are in place because they duplicate, and that is the key to success. It really doesn't matter what works the best, it is what duplicates the easiest and fastest. Simplicity is key!

Develop a plan with your mentor. First, make your names list. Who do you know? Who do you know who is already a Network Marketer? Who do you know who is in the field that your product or service serves? Who do you know who could use your product or service? Who do you want to attract to your organization? What qualities are you looking for in a person?

Decide who you want to attract to your business and become that person. Like attracts like! If you want someone who is goal orientated, organized, ambitious, energetic, compassionate and coachable, you have to become that person. You will not be able to attract successful people into your organization unless you at least possess the qualities that they have. Sponsor Up!

Now go talk to people. I learned from Eric Worre, author of *GO PRO*, that your first 90 days in business can provide you with 90% of your residual income. Do a 90 Day Blitz of all-out, massive action, and you will find your leaders. If you talk to two people a day (10 per week), two out of the 10 will join you. It takes about 100 presentations to get 20 people to join your organization. During your 90 Day Blitz, you will need to talk to a lot more people to get 20 per month. Recruit at least 60 people into your organization, and at the end of the, year approximately 12 will still be in your organization doing something, eight will be sharing the business, four will be leaders, and one will be a 'Rock Star,' providing about 90% of your income.

If you sponsor one person at a time, they will not see the big picture or potential of this amazing opportunity of Network Marketing. Sponsor in groups, and they will feel a sense of community. They will work together and rise together. Make it a goal to do a 90 Day Blitz each year. Your leaders will emerge, and you will have a solid business with a passive, residual income.

Duck, Duck, Goose!

Mark A. Sterling

No matter how good – or not so good we were at Duck, Duck, Goose, we all remember this classic childhood game. A group of players sit in a circle, facing inward, while another player, who is "it", walks around tapping or pointing to each player in turn, calling each a "duck" until finally calling one a "goose" (or a "gray duck" in Minnesota). The "goose" then rises and tries to tag "it", while "it" tries to return to and sit where the "goose" had been sitting. If "it" succeeds, the "goose" becomes "it" and the process begins again. If the "goose" tags "it", the "goose" may return to sit in the previous spot and "it" resumes the process.

Well, here is the question. Are you ready to be "It"? Are you ready to lead? Are you ready to be put up front...to create the culture, the systems?

When people give up on wanting to follow you – you lose your business.

Being 'It' (a leader) is different as an entrepreneur than as supervisor or manager at a traditional job. Most jobs are based on time - not results.

Here are some 'It' insights

- The most important part of the day is leadership training.
- The quality and quantity of your business is in direct proportion to your leadership.
- Just because a person means business doesn't mean that they're mean.
- In creating dramatic wealth, being highly dependent doesn't work.
- You cannot attain financial independence by being full. You MUST be hungry.

"It" insights cont.

- Leadership copies consistency and work ethic, others copy how people dress, speak and what they have.
- Never be in competition with others, because very few people operate in excellence.
- Never fake being on fire.
- Don't confuse consensus with accuracy.
- When your caller ID rings it shouldn't read a name – it should display their goals.
- Volume up or down is temporary. Sincerity is permanent.
- Go to where the solution is – don't expect the solution to come to you.
- If you stack bricks to build the tallest building and leave out the mortar, it will fall.

Lead From the Front

Carole Cheatam

As you advance in positions in MLM, you're required to take on a leadership role with the idea of helping others also gain in position, thereby creating more leaders. Throughout my extensive career prior to the MLM industry, I had held many leadership positions. So, I was never concerned about the task, especially since we were all independent business owners. Although I felt very confident that I was doing a great job leading my team, I soon found out I wasn't leading at all. You see, there's a fine line between leading and managing, and I had become a very effective manager. I had begun to spend the majority of my time training, focusing on administrative tasks, creating promotions, and countless other (what we in the industry call) non-income producing activities. I was relieved to find out that it's not uncommon for leaders in the industry to assume a managing role.

We were so blessed to have John Maxwell mentor the leaders in our company, so I had the good fortune of learning from this great man just what comprised a great leader. I keep this quote from John in my head and in my heart, "A leader is one who knows the way, goes the way, and shows the way." I immediately got it....I knew the way, and I was showing the way, but I was no longer going the way. My recruiting had taken a back seat to showing others how to recruit; how could I possibly ask my team to do what I was not doing? I apologized to my team and assured them that I was climbing down into the trenches with them. But even before I made that transition, I spoke with each team member to discuss their expectations of me, and my expectations of them; another very valuable lesson learned from John Maxwell.

I wish I could say that I've never slipped into management mode again, but I'm so much more aware when I do, and I have John Maxwell's quote to remind me of my responsibility as a leader.

The Only Way to Lose is to Quit

Carole Cheatam

When I started this journey, I had no idea how challenging it would be at times. Oh, I understood it was a business, but seriously, how hard could this be? I bet that's the mistake that many people make when they join the direct sales industry. When you're building a team or establishing a customer base, you have a vested interest in those individuals. Each one of the promoters has made a financial commitment for a reason that's very important to them. Their goal may be to add a little extra income to their family or to replace the income from lost employment. Whatever the reason, it is very important to them that they experience some success, and they look to their leaders to help facilitate that success. But when the success doesn't come as quickly as they like it, they may choose to leave. Others may decide that it's more work than they anticipated, so they may choose to move on. And often a friend of a friend will convince them there's a better company with better products and it's just the right opportunity for them....again, they may opt to leave.

Observing people come and go...and sometimes seeing more go than come....became very worrisome to me and I sought counsel from my mentors. They provided me with very sound advice and helped allay my fears. They explained that it's the nature of the business, and reminded me that in traditional corporate businesses there is also turnover. Without a doubt we experience more turnover in this industry than probably any other, but at the end of the day, each person had to make the decision to be successful or not be successful. This isn't rocket science...it's one of the few industries which will compensate you based on the work you perform. Just remember that if you're not challenged, you're not growing. So my advice would be to just be still.....you only lose if you quit.

Success Leaves Clues

Jody P. Humphrey

The beauty of the direct sales industry is that there are so many people that have had success that you can mirror. You have to do what winners do and follow their success. One of the main reasons people are drawn to direct sales is that there is a system to follow. Regardless of the product or service, the principles of success in multi-level marketing are the same. You are in the building business—whether building your team or your customer base.

All direct sales companies have a system. You must be system driven—know the system and work the system. Duplication equals success. Most successful teams in direct sales are based on great products. Adding team members alone will not guarantee a successful career in direct sales. You need team members and personal sales. If you use the business building system provided and you talk to enough people success is inevitable—both in team members and sales.

The law of numbers is a big part of success especially in direct sales. If you meet and talk to enough people either one-on-one or through networking you will find interested people. All roads lead to new customers and new team members. You have to continually be building your list—your list of potential brand partners and your list of potential customers. You have to write down the list--this makes it real. Your list is ever-changing, ever evolving. As you build your list through networking make sure you are writing those new names down. Your list is your business plan—it's your life-line and if it remains stagnant your business remains stagnant too.

Your goals also have to be written. Written goals have much more power than just your words. You must stretch your vision. Where there is great vision there is great success. You must see what can be, not just what is, both for you and your team. All great direct sales leaders have the vision, coupled with action and the ability to motivate their team to follow them. Success is a system—follow the clues and follow the success.

Excel at Edification

Carol D. Neal

My last direct sales company taught me to respect the power of edification, and my mentors in that company had raised it to an art form. Edification is the act of lifting up a person you are introducing to someone, speaking highly of them and most importantly, building up his or her credibility. The purpose is NOT to stroke that person's ego or to impress the audience, whether the audience is one person or many, but rather to impress UPON the audience the importance of listening to what that person has to say, to get them excited and looking forward to meeting or hearing from that person, and to help them identify with the person.

This is especially important when you are presenting someone in your upline to a prospect. Your prospect may not know you well at all, or even if they do, they may trust you personally but perhaps not on a business basis (especially if they are friends or family who know you have no experience yet in the industry and haven't yet made any money!) If you properly edify your upline as an expert the prospect will respect them, or at the very least, know that the expert knows more than you. They will feel they are getting the message from a credible source. And it actually reflects better on you that you were humble enough to reach out to an expert. This applies to 3 way calls, two-on-one meetings in person, or when you are introducing a prospect to someone at a company event.

Here's an example of how I would do a confirmation to set up a 3 way call or meeting, or even to get a prospect excited about the speaker at an event...I'd do the edification BEFORE we get together, I want to get them excited to meet the expert, and I'd use a formula I first heard about from Mr. Mark Sterling, who is also an author in this book. You want to appeal to the four types of people that may be in your audience, so think about it like you're going fishing in the ocean: A Shark is all about the money; a Whale is all about the community; an Urchin is all about the research, and a Dolphin is all about the fun.

"Sam, I can't wait for you to meet my business partner and mentor, Ms Tracee Randall. She and her husband Bobby were small business owners and were very successful in another networking company before they started focusing on Organo. In their very first month in the company, they hit the first Executive Level of Sapphire with over $20,000 in sales, and they have now advanced to Ruby which means their monthly volume is now equal to the sales of 1-2 Starbucks! They are concentrating on helping me and others reach our goals. Tracee knows all the facts and is passionate about helping people with their health and finances, and she is loads of fun, too, you're really going to like her. I have asked for just a few moments of her time, so I'll just introduce you quickly when I get her on the line."

So to attract all four types of people (if I don't know which one Sam is), in the above example I gave specifics about Tracee's level of success (to interest the Shark), her passion for helping others (to engage the Whale), her knowledge (to satisfy the Urchin) and mentioned that she is fun (to excite the Dolphin).

A skilled upline will in turn back-edify you...back or cross-edification is the act of giving back edification to someone who has already edified you. It creates a positive team atmosphere, and in the case of an expert edifying the team member who just edified them to the prospect, it elevates the status of the team member in the eyes of their prospect and lowers the natural barriers that we as humans put up.

Why the People You Think Will Say Yes, Say No

Dannella Burnett

If you've ever tried a Direct Sales or MLM company, you know that moment when you tried the product, used the service or saw the opportunity and said "YES"! Then you immediately thought of the folks you know that you were so excited to share with and just KNEW that they would all say "YES" immediately...but then, they said "No", and in some cases it was "NO" and "NO NO NO NO NO!!!"

Why does that happen? Why don't they see the incredible opportunity that you see? Why aren't they as excited as you are to try this product that will bring them (better health, weight loss, beautiful skin, the right accessory, more fun....insert the main benefit of your product)? Why aren't they your first recruits and your first customers?

You've probably read that sales are largely a result of the right mindset. That is the truth. Your right mindset AND your customer or prospect's right mindset. The truth is our closest friends and family have a mindset about us that goes back for some time. They've often seen us at our worst, our most immature, our least businesslike and our least leadership acting. They have a preconceived notion of us that may need to be RESET before they are willing to invest in US. Yes, you are sharing a product or company, but truly you are asking them to invest in YOU first. And they may need to see you in action before their hope that you do well translates to opening their wallet to see you do well and play a part.

So does this mean you should skip the family and friends? I don't think so. I think that sharing your product or opportunity with friends and family can be a great way to practice your sales presentation or a great place to sample your products and get feedback. But keep in mind that whether they say "yes" or "no" won't be the deciding factor on your success in the Direct Sales Industry. Even if they ALL say yes, you will be sharing with new people that you meet or seek out and your net worth will be determined by your network beyond family and friends.

Once your family and friends see that you have some success and their MINDSET about you changes, and they see you as the successful business person you are becoming or as the rest of the world sees you, or as YOU see you, many friends and family members may take a second look at information you may have long ago shared the first time. Bottom line, when you have a dream or believe in a product – GO FOR IT! Share with all, accept that their yes or no alone won't determine your future and keep on growing and sharing.

WHY?

Susan Guthrie

A person's WHY is their reason for doing what they do. It is the purpose behind their actions. If the job is hard, you will do it anyway if your WHY is strong enough.

When asked why they take a traditional job, most people say that they need the money. They are okay with being motivated by money when there is no risk involved. Their reputation is not on the line. They don't have to tell themselves what to do each day and they have a guaranteed salary. It is comfortable.

But, is money really the best motivator for a Network Marketing Business? Probably not. Your WHY has to be bigger than money to motivate you past the inevitable "Wall Kicking Moments," as Susan Sly calls them. We will all face the naysayers and hear the negative comments about Network Marketing. *"You have to get in early to make any money. " "Only the ones at the top make anything."*

We will all have disappointments. Some people will say yes and never do anything. Some of the people we know and love turn their backs on us and won't even listen to how great our products are. Your WHY has to be bigger than money to pick you up when you get knocked down.

Your WHY will typically evolve as your business grows. Your first WHY might be that your family needs a car for transportation. As you grow in your self-confidence and in your Network Marketing Business, your WHY becomes bigger. What means more to you than anything else? What brings tears to your eyes when you talk about it? What will make you get up early and stay up late to talk to people about your business or opportunity? What will challenge you get out of your comfort zone to talk to total strangers? Your WHY has to be big enough to overcome all obstacles, because they will come before the money does.

Of course, your WHY can be about money, but not just about earning money. What will it mean for your family when you have financial freedom? What does that look like? Is your home paid for? Can you cover the cost of college for your children and grandchildren? Would traveling around the world in first class excite you? Would staying home with your children mean the world to you? Whatever it is, write it down! Tell your family and friends WHY you have chosen your company and Network Marketing. Be proud of it!

Eric Worre says that with Network Marketing, you will become a better person, face fears, solve problems, fuel your mind with positivity, grow stronger and learn to lead. The greatest gift isn't what you get – it's who you become in the process. Life is a journey with Network Marketing. Enjoy the ride!

What is the fastest way to get everything that you want? It is in serving and giving that we receive. Jen Smith said, "Find what you love and SERVE it with focus and commitment."

"Success is not the result of making money; making money is the result of success—and success is in direct proportion to our service. Most people have this law backwards. They believe that you're successful if you earn a lot of money. The truth is that you can only earn money after you're successful," said Earl Nightingale.

To become successful in Network Marketing, find your WHY. Start loving those around you, serve with an open heart and you will find a life filled with love and abundance. Remember, it is not just about the money – it is about who you become and how you can help others with the money that matters.

Slow Down to Go Fast

JoBeth Martin

I have had the privilege of being trained by industry expert and bestselling author of the "Slight Edge", Jeff Olson. One of the things that Jeff teaches often is, "Slow Down to Go Fast." To be honest, in the beginning I really didn't understand what he meant. It seemed frustratingly inconsistent with other things I was encouraged to do.

With any entrepreneurial adventure you are setting goals and making plans and especially in an MLM business the goals and plans seem to be set for you. It feels a bit like you are on a race to see who can get there the fastest. So how can I slow down to go fast?

One of the very first things I would encourage anyone to do it is find your own "WHY". In other words, what is your motivation for doing a business? What are your truly personal dreams and desires? If you do not know your own personal dreams and set goals accordingly you will likely fail. Worse yet, you may work hard, do everything you are told and meet every deadline and find in the end that you were so busy living someone else's dream by reaching those goals that you are actually further away from your own personal dreams. You reach a goal but you didn't accomplish what you set out to do. A verse of Scripture comes to mind as I type this. In Proverbs 14:1 it says, "A wise woman (or man) builds her house but a foolish one tears it down with her own hands." If you are not taking the time to work through this process and be honest with yourself you could very well be tearing down the very house you want to build, which is your life and dreams for your family.

Once you know your "why" or the driving motivation for what you want to accomplish then you are ready to set some goals. If you are with an MLM, most likely there are goals in place for you to run for. Ask yourself, do I really want to reach those goals and are they consistent with the other goals and dreams in my life? Your company is setting

229

those goals because they know it will help you succeed. Just be sure that you define what success looks like for you.

Once you go through the process of defining your why and figuring out which goals will help you get there, then you are almost ready to run your race. Now decide what the boundaries are for your race. What are the things that will keep you on the right path? They may be a commitment to the system that the company has put into place and an effort to consistently take advantage of training provided. You may set a schedule of when you will be available to work and when you need family and private time. Yes, I said it. You can choose to not work all the time just because it is expected of you. Remember, run your race according to your own goals and dreams. Don't run so fast that you are tearing down your life more quickly than you are building it.

In other words, be intentional. Work hard and well when you work. Then play or rest hard when you are taking a break. For the entrepreneur it is a marathon that is made up of a lot of sprints but you can't be sprinting all the time. Be all in for your life and your business. Only you can decide what that will look like to SLOW DOWN TO GO FAST.

Get Rich Quick and Go Broke Quicker

Carole Cheatam

Often when I'm asked to address a group, I eagerly tell this story. Forty plus years ago an acquaintance of my husband's stopped by to speak to us about this company he had just joined. He was so excited because he was going to sell these products and become rich. And for a very small investment, we could join up with him and get rich too. To entice us even more, he left us with a bottle of laundry/all-purpose cleaner and assured me that once I saw how effective this cleaner was, we'd be jumping up and down to join him. Well I did use the cleaner in my laundry and seeing no suds I was convinced that the product wasn't any good and the company probably wasn't legitimate either. Needless to say, that gentleman went on to become very comfortable financially, and that company is almost a $10 billion company.

So, what happened there? Was it his presentation or my perception? His presentation was right on the mark. He knew the product, he left me with a sample of the product, he was excited, and confident that he was going to be successful. However, in all honesty, when he said he was going to be rich selling an all-purpose cleaner, I immediately thought it's one of those get rich schemes and they don't work!!

Although our industry is perceived by many as a get rich quick scheme, those of us who are a part of the industry know that is far from the truth. I have friends in the industry that are multi-millionaires, but some have been in the industry 20 and 30 years. And, yes, there are some who have visions of grandeur and wealth when they join a network marketing company. They imagine themselves driving the Maserati, living in the 14 bedroom mansion, and taking expensive and elaborate vacations. They want it all, and they want it now. I've seen people jump in and quickly run to the top of the compensation plan because they entice recruits with the promise of making a lot of money and living large. The problem occurs when the people recruited don't attain the success as quickly as they think they should and they quit. So now, you've lost your team, your credibility, and your income has just taken a nosedive.

To build a strong business, you must first choose the company that's the best fit for you. Choose a company whose management team is innovative, accessible and committed to the success of the company.

Make sure the products or services fit your lifestyle. You can't very well sell or promote something that you're not using.

Make sure the compensation plan allows for growth for everyone, you, your team above you and the team you'll build.

Most if not all companies have the technology and training geared to your success; keep abreast of any new roll-outs and be an active participant in the training that's available.

And lastly, be committed to the success of others before your own success.

"You will get all you want in life, if you help enough other people get what they want." ~Zig Ziglar

Follow the System

Susan Guthrie

Definition of System: A set of principles or procedures according to which something is done; an organized scheme or method.

Use the tools - You don't have to be an expert to be successful in a Network Marketing business. Use the tools that the company provides for you. Don't reinvent the wheel. Network Marketing companies spend a lot of money and time developing systems for their associates to use to become successful. It is tempting for new associates to develop their own way to do things, but there is a purpose behind the systems already in place. It is not about what works, it is all about what duplicates. The company website will have tutorials on how to build a successful business. Take the time to study them and train your team to do the same.

There is a common saying in Network Marketing that "You can't say the wrong thing to the right person." That may or may not be true. You need to get educated about your products, company and the Network Marketing Industry so that you know where to find the information to answer questions that are asked. Listen to these questions, and know how to find the answer. Is it best to go to the website for the answer? Would a conference call with an expert be better?

Sometimes, it is best NOT to know the answer to everything. If you know answers and share the details about everything, it might overwhelm potential customers and associates. Don't answer questions that they don't ask. If they ask about the taste of a product, you don't have to tell them everything about the product. Just tell them that it tastes good.   Refer them to the company website for specific information on what is in the product and how the product works. Remember use the tools – that is what is duplicable.

Spend time to train the new associates that you recruit with the tools to allow them to become independent. Don't do everything for them. Empower them to be their own business leaders.

Stay connected with your entire organization via Facebook, newsletters, email, text message, etc. Work with those who raise their hands, show up and really want to be successful. Match energy with energy. Don't spend too much time with those who need it; spend your valuable time with those who want it. As leaders, we have all been guilty of wanting our business or products for others because we see how much they need it. However, until they acknowledge their need and take action, it is a waste of your time to chase them.

Give assignments or specific paths to your associates with a deadline. Assist new members to enroll their first customer, get a first commission, attend their first company event, meet other successful people in the company, get to a new level and get recognized for their effort.

Recognize your team members when they accomplish even the small things; celebrate them on their way to success. Many people in traditional businesses will leave them because they feel under-appreciated by their boss or company, and they will do the same in Network Marketing.

Don't assume that they know how much you love and appreciate them. Let them know! Post congratulations on Facebook, send them a card or note, call them with a successful mentor from your team or send flowers or gifts.

Always keep your team's best interest first. Do what is right for them even if it is not in your best interest. Zig Ziglar says "You can have everything in life that you want if you will just help enough people get what they want." Encourage your team to follow the systems and their dreams.

More Valuable Than Money!

Tracee Randall

The direct sales industry has taken its "hits" over the years, and that is mainly because of the perceived promise it makes to "get rich quick". Can someone "get rich" in the direct sales industry? That's the million dollar question. The answer has to be "YES"—there are hundreds of people who have been able to acquire a fortune in the industry—every company has its rags-to-riches story which inspires others to want to come aboard—it's the great American dream! Statistically, in fact, more millionaires have been created from the direct sales industry than any other. "Network marketing is looking to be the #1 Millionaire Producing Industry in the world this year and for many years in the future" according to BusinessForHome.org. However, the truth of the matter is this: the AVERAGE person in the industry who commits to building will earn between $500-$1000 per month with consistency and dedication. We have all heard the stats—an additional $500 would help most Americans avoid bankruptcy, so the industry has its merits!

So, with the truth exposed—most people will NOT earn even the coveted 6-figure income in the industry, how is it that we can build a strong, powerful, happy team—and more importantly how can we keep them?! Well, frankly, there is something that is incredibly more valuable than money, and if a leader will take hold of it and give it freely and often to his team, the team will never, ever leave! I wish I had learned this and mastered this early on in my direct sales career—and it does not just ring true in the MLM industry, but in every aspect of our lives. We work in teams in many arenas—our family is our team, our business (whether direct sales or not), our church, our organizations, our networking group, our neighborhood. What is it that we can do that will empower our team members to remain faithful during the good times and the bad? What is it that we as LEADERS can do to ensure that our team will support each other even when they aren't making the money they wanted to make? It's so simple, yet most bosses, most leaders, most business owners completely miss it. The currency that keeps people faithful to any cause is this: RECOGNITION.

The biggest mistake that I have witnessed in the direct sales industry is when the leader fails to recognize the small goals that have been reached. I have been guilty of this as well—and part of the problem is sometimes the leader wants so badly to be recognized themselves that they fail to see that their success comes not from their own efforts, but from the efforts of the hundreds of people who are following! The company that recognizes the seemingly insignificant success of one of its members is the company that WINS! A direct sales company that comes to mind which exemplifies this concept is one called "It Works". It Works is a company which specializes in a "miraculous body wrap" that melts inches of fat away in 45-minutes (hey- it DOES WORK!) as well as a whole line of supplements. What I have witnessed is a perfect example of teamwork—the company itself brands their team members in bright, jazzy lime-green, glitter and sequins—the It Works team is easily recognized in the market-place and that's just for starters. But more important than the glitz and glitter is the way the leadership EDIFIES and recognizes each team member. They get a new customer, the whole world knows! They are promoted on social media, edified in person at meetings, and they make sure each team member is honored for every new step taken—they are great at it! While other direct sales companies are parading the handful of millionaires across stages around the world, this company realizes that it's the hundreds and hundreds of women who are made to feel important, who are recognized by the leadership, that make the company what it is!

If your company doesn't have a built-in recognition program (or even if it does!), then MAKE YOUR OWN! YOU are the leader of your team. How can you recognize them for a job-well-done? Private and public recognition are key components to loyalty of a team member. The great news is this—when you recognize them they will strive to do better, to get better, to work harder—and everyone WINS! What's more valuable than money?? Recognition! Get good at it and see what happens!

INDEX OF TIPS
BY EXPERT

"One good mentor can be more informative than
a college education and more valuable than
a decade's income."

~ Sean Stephenson

AFTERWORD

There are literally hundreds of books and training programs available that will help the small business owner and entrepreneur increase their profits and build their business. It's never in the reading about these ideas and strategies, but in the IMPLEMENTATION of them, that the money flows! It's making the decision to put these principles and concepts into ACTION that makes the difference! Even as we were putting this project together, editing and re-editing, we were excited about what we had in our hands, and even more excited about putting it into the hands of thousands of others in whose lives it will make a difference – IF you choose to take action!

The experts who have joined us in this first edition of #InsiderTips have collectively put together one of the best resource guides that we've seen, and they have given us so much more value than we ever imagined. This process has been an incredible learning experience for us and we are grateful for each and every one of these experts who went the extra mile to provide you, our reader, with the information you need to grow YOU and your business.

There is so much more that we would like to share, so many other incredible experts who can help us—iron sharpens iron—so we will be expanding this into a series of #InsiderTips collaborations. As entrepreneurs we realize that a published work is the new business card—and we have seen the truth of this in our own business, Atlanta Business Spotlight. And just as your business card represents your standard of professionalism and is a reflection of you and your brand, the same holds true with a publication. Our goal with the #InsiderTips series is to offer small business owners and entrepreneurs the opportunity to collaborate with others and be showcased in a high quality volume of work that you can be proud to share. Contact us for information on being part of our next collaboration, so that you too can #BeTheVoice that stands out from the crowd!   Tracee and Carol

Other Programs and Publications available from Atlanta Business Spotlight

'Get MAD About Cancer'
'Make Up Your Mind'
'The FASTest Way to God's Favor and Blessing'
'The Voice That Changed Everything: A Book of Gratitude'
'Insider Tips 2: 115 Innovative Ways To Increase Profit'

Also available:
The incredible Instatricity phone charger mentioned several times in this book!

Find all of these and more at:
www.TraceeRandall.com
Use Promo Code "InsiderTips" and save!